The MYTH of the RICH CANADIAN DOCTOR

The MYTH of the RICH CANADIAN DOCTOR

DOCTOR, WHAT IS THE STATE OF YOUR FINANCIAL HEALTH?

A CANDID CONVERSATION ABOUT
A TABOO TOPIC FROM ONE DOCTOR TO ANOTHER

MICHAEL VARENBUT, MD, MBA
VICKI RACKNER, MD FACS

THE MYTH OF THE RICH CANADIAN DOCTOR
DOCTOR, WHAT IS THE STATE OF YOUR FINANCIAL HEALTH?

©2019 Michael Varenbut, MD, MBA

©2017, 2019 Vicki Rackner, MD, FACS

All Rights Reserved.

No part of this publication may be reproduced or distributed in any form or by any means, or stored in a database retrieval system without prior written permission of the copyright holder.

The concept of pain personalities is a trademark of Vicki Rackner, MD.

www.theMythoftheRichDoctor.ca

Published by Michael Varenbut, Toronto, Canada

ISBN (Ppk):   978-1-9991531-0-6

ISBN (ebook): 978-1-9991531-1-3

Material in this book is for educational purposes only. Neither the publisher nor the author assumes any liability for any errors or omissions, or for how this book's contents are used or interpreted, or for any consequences resulting directly or indirectly from the use of this book. For legal advice or any other, please consult your personal attorney or appropriate professional.

10 9 8 7 6 5 4 3 2 1

CONTENTS

Introduction: Physicians and Money................1

PART I: PHYSICIANS' FINANCIAL HEALTH

1: Are Doctors Rich?............................9

What Does It Mean to Be Rich?
What's the Difference between Being Rich and Being Wealthy?
Why Is Building Wealth Important?
Thriving Physicians versus Struggling Physicians
Physicians' Financial Truth
Money as a Taboo Topic
Lessons from Our Patients
The Investing Landscape Is Changing
The Systems Problem

2: Your Financial Health........................31

What Is Your Current State of Financial Health?
What Is Your Pain Personality?
How Do You Make Financial Choices?
What Is Your Mind-set about Money?

3: Your Objective Financial Picture..................49

Your Financial Vital Signs
Are You on Track?
What Is the Path to Financial Freedom?

PART II: GENERATING MORE EARNED INCOME

4: The New Thriving Medical Practice: Working Smarter—Not Harder 59

Your Income

Times Are Changing

Do You Run a Small Business?

Do You Need Sales and Marketing Skills?

Are You Ready for Money to Enter the Doctor-Patient Relationship?

How Do Physicians Overcome the Professional and Ethical Barriers to Business Success?

5: Are You Leaving Money on the Exam Table? 77

Failure to Negotiate Contracts

Failure to Collect What You're Owed for Clinical Services

Failure to Negotiate Terms of Loans

Failure to Scrutinize Expenses

Failure to Minimize Your Taxes

Being Penny-Wise and Pound-Foolish

Failure to Harness the Power of Leverage

Failure to Protect against Fraud and Embezzlement

6: Ten Ways to Generate More Revenue 89

1. Moonlight
2. Focus
3. Leverage Staff
4. Add Clinical Services
5. Change Practice Settings
6. Consider Moving
7. Educate, Empower, and Entertain
8. Coach and Consult
9. Assume Physician Leadership
10. Start a Company

What's Right for You?

Income Is Just the Start

PART III: PUTTING YOUR MONEY TO WORK AND GETTING BETTER RETURNS ON YOUR INVESTMENTS

7: A New Wealth-Building Approach. 113

Wealth Building Is an Epic Task

The Threats to Your Wealth

8: The Ten Financial Habits of Wealthy Physicians.......129

Do You Practice Habits of Wealth?   Ask the Best Questions
What is Your Path to Wealth?   Answer Day-to-Day Questions

Afterword: A Call to Action......................151

Acknowledgments.............................153

About the Authors.............................155

INTRODUCTION: PHYSICIANS AND MONEY

Are you in a financial position to do what you want to do when you want to do it? Could you afford to invest in your medical practice, take time off to care for a sick family member, or make a substantial donation to your favorite cause?

This book is your invitation into a frank conversation about physicians' ultimate taboo topic: money.

Why dive into the discomfort? Just as gas fuels your car and oxygen fuels your cells, money fuels your life. Every choice you make carries financial consequences. The scarcity or abundance of money drives purchasing choices. Money enters into decisions about whether to volunteer in a medical mission, bring in a new partner, or launch a blog.

Further, many physicians in private practice—perhaps even you—find themselves at a crossroads contemplating big changes to position themselves for success in a rapidly changing medical landscape. A solid and secure financial foundation gives you more options.

As multiple studies have shown, there is a strong link between financial health, physical health, and mental health. It is our hope that by setting a foundation for strong financial health among physicians, a myriad of benefits will follow.

What Is This Book About?

The goal of this book is simple. We want to help you see a more hopeful future.

This means breaking the conspiracy of silence and telling the truth about physicians' ultimate taboo topic—physicians and their relationship with money.

The ideas in this book are intended as a therapeutic intervention to alleviate the suffering of physicians imprisoned by the pandemic of despair. We know this sounds dramatic. However, think about the conversations you have with your colleagues. Take a look at the critically high rates of physician burnout.

Many physicians with whom we speak experiences acute financial pain, regardless of his or her income. Earning less hurts, no matter how much you make. Paying ever-increasing taxes hurts. Worries about market volatility keep physicians up at night, regardless of the size of their port-folio.

Financial security—and financial insecurity—impact every dimension of a physician's life. Con-structing a firm financial foundation is the first step toward achieving the personal and professional goals that attracted you to a career in medicine. Wealth gives you the freedom to do what you want to do, when you want to do it.

In this book we'll explore

- The forces that shape physicians' relationship with money,
- Common financial mistakes physicians make,
- Habits that separate wealthy physicians from struggling physicians,

- A process to assess your financial health and a plan to work toward greater wealth, and

- Financial concerns unique to physicians.

This is not your standard primer on investment strategies. Here you'll see how you can apply the principles, skills, and tools that help you take care of patients to make consistent, informed financial choices. Let's develop financial standards of care for your money that parallel clinical standards of care for your patients.

This book is meant to be a start to a long journey and a relationship that you will build with your "dream team," in navigating the rough waters of personal finance and investment.

You optimize your financial health and build wealth the same way you manage your patients' medical care.

Here's Dr. Rackner's Story

I've made virtually every financial mistake you will read about. I've trusted the wrong people. I've lost money in DDDs—dumb doctor deals. I've mismanaged money by not knowing what I didn't know, or acting on things I thought I knew that turned out to be wrong.

So why read this book?

Over the past twenty-five years, I've indulged my intense curiosity about physicians and their relationship with money.

You will benefit from trends I identified by personally listening to money stories of many physicians on all ends of the wealth spectrum. You'll see what I've learned about the financial habits that separate the wealthy physicians from the struggling physicians.

You will also benefit from what I have learned through working with many professional financial advisors who hire me to learn more about physicians' financial needs.

Here's Dr. Varenbut's Story

I have wanted to become a physician for as long as I can remember, going back to at least the age of six. Through many years of hard work, dedication, and commitment, I was able to gain a position as a medical student at the University of Toronto and graduate with honours, while being one of the youngest students in my class. Over the twenty-five years that followed, I had practiced medicine in multiple clinical disciplines and have managed to successfully create multiple medical clinics and entities in the process. Being a serial entrepreneur, I have always thrived on building and creating innovative organizations that brought value to multiple stakeholders.

Growing up poor, I became interested in the financial world in my late teens and dedicated many hours to learning about investments, financial security, and the world of economics, in addition to always staying current with medical developments. More recently, I returned to school, and obtained an MBA from Ivey at Western University. Combining the unlikely worlds of health care and entrepreneurship have become my newfound passion.

At this new stage in my life, I swore that anything I would set my mind to do in the future would have to be in line with the following three questions: What am I deeply passionate about? What taps my talent? and What meets a significant need in the world?

Having come across the Myth of the Rich Doctor, and meeting Dr. Vicki Rackner, it became crystal clear to me that our collaboration on a Canadian version of the book would satisfy all three of the above set questions.

Having firsthand knowledge of the Canadian health care system, as well as Canada's economic environment, I was also keenly aware that many Canadian physicians have never had the luxury of an education that included finance, business, and economics.

Throughout my medical career, I was also deeply and passionately involved in medical education at multiple levels, from undergraduates to practicing physicians. With a strong academic interest, I was part of the University of Toronto faculty of medicine staff for twelve years and achieved a rank of assistant professor. It is from this perspective that I hope to fulfill a missing gap, which will hopefully benefit many physicians, their families, and the public at large.

How This Book Is Organized

You will find three sections of the book, organized somewhat like a history and physical.

In Part I you will explore financial health. First, you will see how well physicians as a group do. Are doctors, in fact, rich? Then it's time to focus on you. What is your current state of financial health? What are your financial goals, and are you on track to get there?

In Part II, you will learn ideas about how you can optimize your revenue while honouring the integrity of the doctor-patient relationship.

In Part III, you will learn the habits that separate wealthy physicians from struggling physicians. You will see the most common financial mistakes physicians make.

I have tried to add a uniquely Canadian perspective as much as possible, and recognizing the tremendous work that Dr. Rackner has done in the American version, I have kept many of her storys, vignettes, and insights. Much of medicine is universal, yet living in Canada brings with it a wealth of variances.

We physicians would never offer a diagnosis or a treatment plan to patients we have not personally examined. That could be negligent. Similarly, you want to get your financial advice from a team of professionals that offers you a considered plan based on a complete evaluation. The insights in this book will hopefully point you in the direction of building greater wealth and making a bigger impact.

It's Never Too Late

ou may have made financial choices in the past you regret. We would like to help you replace judgment with compassion, understanding, and a prudent plan. There are reasons you made the choices you did.

At a recent conference that I [Dr. Varenbut] attended, the MaRS Healthkick, a very astute CEO of a private equity firm that invests in health care stated, "It's not that AI is going to replace doctors, it's doctors that use AI that are going to replace those that don't." I feel similarly about Financial Intelligence or FI and Canadian physicians. To survive and thrive in our health care environment, physicians are going to have to become highly financially intelligent, and it is my goal to help them in this endeavor.

You can make different choices starting today. It's never too late or too early. There is always hope for a better financial tomorrow. Time is money, so let's get started!

ou may have made financial choices in the past you regret. I would like to help you replace judgment with compassion, understanding, and a prudent plan. There are reasons you made the choices you did.

You can make different choices starting today. It's never too late or too early. There is always hope for a better financial tomorrow. Time is money, so let's get started!

PART I

PHYSICIANS' FINANCIAL HEALTH

1 ARE DOCTORS RICH?

How often do you run into people who think that doctors are "made of money"?

PPatients say, "Of course doctors are rich. Just look at the cars in the doctors' parking lot."

Public opinion holds that you deserve to be rich. In conversations about ways to control health care costs, you do not often hear patients say, "Let's cut back on physicians' fees; they're simply getting paid too much."

Family, friends, and causes often turn to physicians first when raising funds.

So, are doctors rich?

Most importantly, what is the state of your financial health?

What Does It Mean to Be Rich?

We lack precision about the words that are the very tools of a conversation about financial health.

We use lay terms like rich and poor and wealthy. These words, like obese, constipated, and demented, mean different things to different people. This makes the difficult money conversation even more challenging.

For purposes of this book, please consider this working definition of rich: If you can comfortably and reliably meet your monthly expenses to support your desired lifestyle, you are rich.

You've heard the expression "house-rich, cash-poor." Let's define poor as the opposite of rich. If you struggle to pay your bills on a monthly basis, or you are dissatisfied with your current lifestyle, you are poor.

issatisfied with your current lifestyle, you are poor.

Feeling Rich, Acting Rich, and Being Rich

There's a difference between feeling rich, acting rich, and being rich.

Feeling rich. Some people say, "I'll feel rich when I make enough money." That's like saying, "I'll smile when I feel happy." You can decide to smile whether or not you're happy, and often become happy by the act of smiling. Similarly, you can decide that today you are satisfied with your standard of living.

People who feel rich tend to compare themselves favorably to others who have less. They experience the world as a place of abundance. People who feel poor tend to compare themselves unfavorably to others who have more.

You can feel rich or poor no matter what's in your investment portfolio. Feeling rich is an inside job; it's about perspective and attitude.

The best way to feel rich is to express gratitude for what you have and give to others less fortunate than you are.

Who Gives More?

Using American IRS data, the Chronicle of Philanthropy found that between 2006 and 2012, the lowest-income Americans increased the percentage of their incomes that they gave to charity. However, as their incomes increased, the percentage they gave to charities decreased.

The Canadian tax law and the CRA has a very generous tax credit system for donors to charities. The Charitable Donations Tax Credit can be up to 29 percent of the amount you donated at the federal level. You may also be entitled to an additional amount reaching up to 24 percent of your donation depending on your province of residence.

Acting rich. Unlike feeling rich, acting rich leaves physical evidence for others to observe. For some, acting rich means living in a huge house, making luxury purchases, or belonging to elite clubs. For others, it means making large and sometimes public donations.

Because doctors earn generous incomes, they can afford to spend more. The more you spend, the richer you may appear to others.

Action Step

Want to feel rich right now? Reach out and help someone less fortunate than you are. Remember, though, *feeling* rich and *being* rich are two different things.

Being rich. Here are the two qualities of physicians who truly are rich:

1. They celebrate what they have and decide that they are satisfied with their current lifestyle.

2. They spend within a designated budget.

The unhappy doctor held hostage by recurrent thoughts such as, "If I only made more money, I would be able to buy that _____ (you can fill in the blank), and then I would be happy," is not rich, no matter how much he makes.

Further, the doctor making seven figures who is losing sleep wondering how he will make payments on his leased Mercedes S550 is not rich.

People who surround themselves with luxury items may look rich and feel rich. However, if they cannot afford their luxury purchases, they are living the myth of the rich doctor.

Being rich is about (1) a relationship between income and expenses; and (2) the level of satisfaction about your current financial reality. You become rich by making choices about your thoughts, your feelings, and your financial actions.

How Do You Compare?

It's easy to look around, see physicians living a more luxurious lifestyle, and say, "I wish I could trade places!"

Please remember three things:

- If you knew what others' lives were really like, you might conclude that you're better off than they are.

- There will always be people with more money than you have.

- You earn more than about 95 percent of Canadians (according to Statistics Canada) and 99 percent of the world's population! (per Investopedia sources).

I've spoken with physicians who tell themselves they don't have enough. They can be as unhappy and as stressed as physicians who cannot pay their bills.

Keep your eyes on your own paper. Live your own life, and let other people live theirs.

How Many Doctors Really Are Rich?

How do you know who is rich and who is poor? We have objective tax data about physicians' incomes. However, income is only part of the story.

The metrics by which being rich is measured include both objective and subjective elements. You become rich by making choices about your thoughts, your feelings, and your financial actions. That means that you will only know with certainty whether or not one individual is rich—yourself!

Based on our conversations with physicians over many years, we can tell you that looks are often deceiving. You cannot distinguish between physicians who are living the myth of the rich doctor and others who are, in fact, rich.

John, a retired cardiothoracic surgeon, projected the very image of success. He owned an exquisitely appointed mansion and vacation home, drove luxury cars, belonged to exclusive clubs, wore designer clothing, and jetted off on exotic vacations.

Yet, upon his death, John's family discovered his shameful secret. He left his wife and children nothing but debt. As they say in Texas, John was "all hat and no cattle."

Mary, on the other hand, lives in a modest house, drives a ten-year-old car, and takes stay-cations instead of going to Europe. She could retire at age fifty if she so chooses. She doesn't look rich, but her frugality and disciplined investing have paid off, literally. She's the millionaire next door.

What's the Difference between Being Rich and Being Wealthy?

Please consider this working definition: **You are wealthy if you can comfortably and reliably meet your monthly expenses to support your desired lifestyle—even if your earned income ended today.** You measure your level of wealth by the duration of time you could sustain your desired lifestyle without earned income. Like it is often said, "Cash flow is king."

Most physicians budget their way to becoming rich and then invest their way to becoming wealthy.

Are Physicians Wealthy?

Physicians' high incomes do not reliably translate to high net worth and the freedom wealth buys. According to the Canadian Institute for Health Information (CIHI), there were more than 84,000 physicians in Canada as of September 2017, or 230 per 100,000 population.

According to the CIHI roughly one third of senior Canadian physicians (those over age sixty-five) are actively engaged in patient care. Some continue to practice medicine because of the ongoing professional rewards.

Consider this conversation overheard at a meeting between two gray-haired surgeons. One said, "Did you hear that Joe died in the OR?"

The other responded, "I didn't know that he was sick!"

The first said, "He wasn't. He was scrubbed and stepped away from the OR table waiting for the frozen section. He just slumped over. They couldn't revive him. Joe always told me that's the way he wanted to go."

Here's the dirty little secret. Many physicians will be economic slaves to their practices well into their retirement years. They are not positioned to replace their earned income with investment income at age sixty-five or even seventy-five.

Several Councils on Medical Education invested resources to explore the complex task of creating guidelines and standards to assess the clinical competency of aging physicians. Even though there are unclear rules with respect to mandatory retirement age for physicians in Canada, the retirement age for physicians may change in the future, and possibly affect your earning potential.

Why Is Building Wealth Important?

Your financial security impacts every part of your personal and professional life:

Financial security opens doors to professional possibilities. Wealth gives you more choices as you consider how you position yourself for success in the political climate of dramatic change.

Financial security helps you avoid distracted doctoring. Money worries serve as a constant source of distraction. Just as you wouldn't text and drive, similarly, you should avoid distractions when treating patients.

Financial security helps you put your family's needs first. A colleague decided to cut back on her ER shifts when her children became adolescents. She knew she wanted to be there to guide her kids through that tricky stage of development. She also knew that she could afford it.

Financial security immunizes you from burnout. Insufficient income is one of the top five risk factors for developing burnout. Further, insufficient savings and debt correlate with burnout.

Financial security helps you treat burnout. You may decide to cut back on your hours, create a specialty focus in your practice, or launch an entrepreneurial venture like writing a blog or building a company around a medical invention you made.

Financial security helps you put the patients' needs first. Removing the constant fear and anxiety over personal financial health is very likely to allow a practicing physician to focus their energy and attention toward caring for their patients.

Financial security helps you leave a legacy and serve in a bigger way. The greater your wealth, the greater impact you can make for your family and for worthy causes you're passionate about.

Thriving Physicians versus Struggling Physicians

Some physicians build significant wealth. Like Mark (not his real name or for that matter any other names here have been masked, the stories are real), a practicing anesthesiologist in his early sixties, who just donated several million dollars to a cancer research organization.

Or Marge, the widow of an ophthalmologist who knows with certainty that she will never outlive her money. In fact, she has paid for all of her grandchildren's post-secondary educations.

Or Jill, a dermatologist in her seventies who continues to see patients. It's not because she has to; she has complete financial security. She volunteers her time at a local clinic and participates in medical missions because she loves her work.

Other intelligent physicians with excellent clinical judgment make poor financial choices. Like the brilliant medical school classmate of Dr. Vicki's who confided that filing for bankruptcy might be his only option after his divorce.

The Reasons Physicians Fail to Build Wealth

What keeps physicians from building wealth? Here are some common reasons usually cited, that we will explore in greater detail:

What keeps physicians from building wealth? Here are some common reasons usually cited, that we will explore in greater detail:

- Medical school debt
- Late start on earning and savings
- Failure to protect assets against known and overlooked risks
- Poor or no tax planning
- Getting investment advice from the wrong people
- Fraud and theft
- Living beyond their means and overspending

This is like saying patients become obese because they eat too many donuts. It may be true, but it fails to tell the whole story.

Further, it fails to lead to sustained solutions that deliver different outcomes. Budgets work about as well as diets.

The Real Causes of Unrealized Wealth

What separates thriving physicians from struggling physicians living the myth of the rich doctor? Do thriving physicians come from wealthier families? Do they begin their careers with less debt? Are they more likely to have an MBA?

Here's the defining difference: Thriving doctors have a healthier relationship with money. They invest time understanding how money works and treat their money with respect. They have clarity about what's most important to them and assure that their financial choices reflect their values. They assemble a team of experts (their dream team) to help them achieve their desired outcomes.

Physicians' failure to build wealth is a symptom of a deeper financial ill—their dysfunctional relationship with money. Physicians as a group are busy, competent people who

- Tend to overestimate their ability to manage money, and underestimate the level of difficulty of the challenge,
- Lack insight about what they do and do not know, and
- Lack awareness about the complexities physicians face as they build wealth

Physicians' Financial Truth

Here is the economic reality you face: Physicians who practiced medicine around the time of the inception of Medicare didn't need to master the money conversation. Admission to medical school was thought of as a golden ticket to wealth. Physicians thought that they could afford to make and recover from big financial mistakes.

For physicians practicing medicine today, the rules are different.

1. **It's harder to make money.** You may see your net income eroded by rising practice expenses, increasing administrative burdens, and falling fees.

2. **It's harder for your money to make money.** A possible slower economic growth and very low interest rate environment means that your investments may not generate the kinds of returns they have in the past.

3. **It's harder to know whom to trust to help you manage your money.** How do you make sense of often contradictory investment recommendations? How can you evaluate investment opportunities and assess the competency of the so-called financial experts?

Physicians Are Top Earners

According to Stats Canada, nine out of the ten top earners in Canada call themselves "doctor." As a group, physicians earn more than 90 to 98 percent of the Canadian population. Further, we get paid doing meaningful work we love; many would work for much less.

Based on the Statistics Canada database for 2018, here's how much the top-earning Canadians make:

Top 0.1%: $826,800

Top 1%: $381,300

Top 5%: $179,800

Top 10%: $134,900

In comparison, the average Canadian physician earned $339,000 (as per the Institute of Health Information, September 2017 report). Please keep in mind the differences that likely exist in the definition of "earnings" vs. net income, when one takes into consideration typical expenses for various professions.

This single fact has a number of natural financial consequences that further set doctors apart from the average Canadian:

- **The financial advice for the average Canadian has limited utility for top earners like you.** Just as medical recommendations change whether your patient is eight or eighty, so, too, financial advice needs to be customized to an individual's unique situation.

- **Physicians fall in high tax brackets.** As you will see, taxes are your single biggest expense. Your ability to proactively manage your taxes determines how quickly you build wealth.

- **Physicians are more likely to be approached for financial support** from relatives, friends, and philanthropic causes.

- **Physicians are recognized as having "deep pockets"** and are named by lawyers in lawsuits in our litigious society.

- **Physicians are more likely to be the targets of scams, fraud, and embezzlement.**

- **Physicians have more investing options open to them,** as they typically qualify as "accredited investors," a point to be discussed further, later.

- **Physicians have easier access to credit** and "other people's money" they can leverage to build wealth.

- **Physicians have more to lose if they become disabled.**

Is It Fair?

How much money should physicians make? How much more should they make than teachers or firefighters or pilots?

Whether or not it's fair or right, physicians do, in fact, earn handsomely. Become a good steward of money so that your wealth allows you to serve in a bigger way.

Here are some truths:

- **Half of doctors are behind in retirement planning.** Many physicians wonder if and when they will ever be able to retire.

- **Half of doctors work with professional financial advisors.** The other half are financial do-it-yourselfers. As a group, physicians who work with the financial experts feel more prepared for retirement.

- **Financial stresses contribute to burnout.**

Many sources and surveys suggested that burnout among Canadian physicians has reached a critical level. While some differences can be seen among provinces and specialties, the overall trend is quite worrisome. Several provincial medical associations have even created special task forces to further address these trends.

While there are multiple causes of physician burnout, many say that insufficient income is one of the top contributing causes

White Coats versus Suits

Physicians have a different relationship with money than business-oriented people.

One of the biggest differences between you—a "White Coat"—and your friends in the business community—let's call them "Suits"—comes down to your relationship with money.

> *In the world of business, money is the metric by which you measure success. Profitability is openly discussed. Businesses invest to learn new ways to become profitable.*

> *In the world of medicine, service is the metric by which we measure success.*

The phrase, "He's focused on profits" can be a compliment or an insult depending on whether you are a Suit or a White Coat.

A Suit would say, "Of course I'm focused on profits. That's what the board and shareholders expect of me. After all, successful businesses generate healthy profits."

A White Coat would be insulted to be described as someone "in it for the money." White Coats want to be known for making a difference in patients' lives.

However, it's not quite that black and white. Neither Suits nor White Coats can afford to focus exclusively on one or the other. Businesses will not be profitable unless they provide value to their customers; clinicians cannot serve patients unless they generate profit to keep the lights on and staff paid. Many Canadians don't realize that their physicians operate a business and are responsible for all its associated expenses.

As you think about building wealth, you are leaving the world of medicine and stepping into the world of business. These two worlds are wired differently, and you are wired differently than Suits.

Consider a recent episode of the reality TV show Shark Tank, which offers insights about the cultural divide.

A doctor entrepreneur entered the Shark Tank asking for a $3 million investment to grow his medical device company selling synthetic cadavers. He painted the picture of an ideal investment opportunity, complete with an innovative product, a huge proven market, and $10 million in sales.

It seemed obvious to viewers, "He could get a five-Shark deal!"

However, things quickly fell apart during Q&A. Here are snippets from the exchange sparked by the Sharks' inquiries about his sales and profits:

Doctor: "We could be making quite a bit of money if I wanted to. I'm not all that interested in the money. It's a tool I use to hire people."

Lori Greiner: "You're not interested in making money?"

Doctor: "It's not my motivation. Medical training is very important. It's a way of saving lives."

Kevin O'Leary: "What about profits? Do you care about this?"

Doctor: "I will at some point."

This entrepreneur left the Shark Tank without a deal.

To build wealth, you are declaring that you do care about money. The reason to care is simple: the bigger your wealth, the bigger your impact

Money as a Taboo Topic

EEvery day, you speak with your patients about topics that cause them discomfort. Dr. Vicki calls them the "embarrassing Ps": peeing, pooping, and procreating. She had a patient literally die of embarrassment. This woman was too embarrassed to tell her doctor about the blood in her stool. By the time the colon cancer that took her life was diagnosed, it was widely metastatic.

We physicians have our own embarrassing P: paying. For us, money is the ultimate taboo topic. And we see the impact on our financial health.

Why Do Physicians Avoid Conversations about Money?

Here are three reasons why most physicians shy away from conversation about money:

1. **The culture of medicine:** Just as the government calls for the separation of church and state, medical ethics calls for a separation between patient care and a patient's ability to pay. Physicians are expected to make medical choices blinded to financial concerns.

2. **Low financial literacy:** Physicians typically get no formal training in business or finances in medical school or residency.

3. **Vulnerability:** In nature, an animal is either predator or prey. Physicians experience themselves as financial prey. We are the targets of frequent pitches by people who want to work with the "rich doctors."

Lessons from Our Patients

Promoting health and building wealth are parallel processes.

Think about patients who say that they want to avoid a second heart attack or lose weight or stop smoking. What percentage of your patients achieves their stated medical goals? What stands in their way? How many patients take their medications as prescribed by you?

Many of those same obstacles apply to physicians who say that they want to build wealth.

Compliance: Patients know they should take their medication as prescribed just as physicians know they should be saving and investing for retirement. Only about half of patients comply with doctors' orders, and only about half of physicians are on track to retire.

Confusion and conflicting advice: Consider the dean welcoming the incoming class on the first day of medical school, saying, "I have some good news and some bad news. The good news is that at least half of what you're about to learn is true. The bad news is that we don't know which half."

What if only half of what we believe to be true about wealth building—or economic recovery—is right?

Patients want to know answers to specific questions like, "Should I eat eggs or not?" or "Should I take supplements, and, if so, what's the right dose of vitamin E?" Physicians want to know, "Should I invest in real estate or not?"

Complexity: A physician friend of Dr. Vicki's was recently diagnosed with breast cancer, and it was not your standard case. For starters, the tumor did not show up on her mammogram. The pathology report delivered surprises. This left many questions about the treatment plan and the protocol for ongoing surveillance.

At virtually every point on the decision tree, her treating physicians could only speculate about the risks and benefits of each alternative.

She read all the medical literature and was left with the question, "How does this information apply to ME?" In the absence of clear right answers, whom should she trust to answer this question?

This reflects our differences in the ability to live with uncertainty, and our beliefs about whether to err on the side of undertreating or overtreating.

Replace "breast cancer treatment" with "your financial plan," and you will see what you, as a physician, are up against as you build wealth.

How much confidence do you have in your current financial plan? Do you have a written financial plan? How well do you tolerate market volatility? How much can you afford to lose?

The conventional wisdom holds that you take big risks for big gains. Would you prefer to err on the side of protecting what you have, or on the side of growing what you have?

Then again, could the conventional wisdom be wrong? Do you really need to take big risks to get big gains

The Investing Landscape Is Changing

You regularly learn about new diagnostic and therapeutic tools that help you get better medical outcomes.

It should be no surprise that the financial tools to build wealth evolve too. Had you ever heard about "loan-default swaps" before 2008, or about ETFs (exchange traded funds) before 1990?

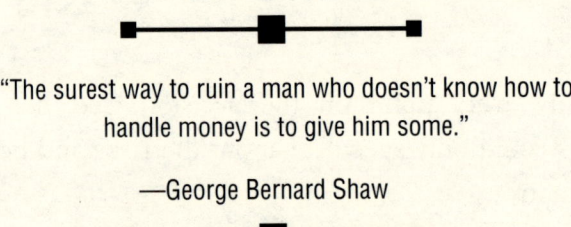

"The surest way to ruin a man who doesn't know how to handle money is to give him some."

—George Bernard Shaw

Financialization of America

Increasingly, the business of North America and the rest of the world is building wealth. In her book Makers and Takers, Rana Foroohar reports that Apple borrowed $17 billion with the intention of leveraging the loan to make money. She said, "The fact that Apple, probably the best-known company in the world and surely one of the most admired, now spends a large amount of time and effort thinking about how to make more money via financial engineering rather than by the old-fashioned kind, tells us how upside down our biggest corporations' priorities have become."

It's not just Apple getting caught up in the trend of "financialization." She also pointed out that airlines can generate more revenue speculating on oil futures than by selling seats. "Dynamic pricing" has become a common practice in the airline industry, as it has in many other sectors.

You are competing with sophisticated investors who have access to ever-more-sophisticated investing products and services.

The Systems Problem

Physicians like yourself face a systems problem in your efforts to build wealth. Wealth building is a complex task. You have a lot to lose—and little time and training to attend to the task. Further, you are competing against savvier investors.

As I spend more time with the financial elite, I see that they play the wealth-building game differently than the average Canadian. It's like the difference between a House League game and the NHL play-offs.

Still, physicians can and do win at the wealth-building game. In Part III of this book, you will see the habits that separate wealthy physicians from struggling physicians.

NOTES

NOTES

NOTES

2 YOUR FINANCIAL HEALTH

What Is Your Current State of Financial Health?

Now let's talk about you and your current state of financial health. Further, let's approach your money as if it were your patient.

First, we'll address your money story. What is your experience with your money? Where does it hurt? What have you tried, and how has that worked for you?

Then we'll look at the objective picture. Last, we'll address how you can assess where you are, define where you would like to be, and make a plan to get there.

Chief Complaint

Today, what is your top money concern? If you had an appointment with a "money doctor," what would your major issue be? Are you doing well and just checking in to assure you're still on the path to financial freedom?

- Are you doing well and just checking in to assure you're still on the path to financial freedom?

- Are you experiencing acute financial pain from a falling income or higher taxes?

- Are you and your partner disagreeing on how money gets saved and spent?

- Are you recovering from a recent financial loss or wanting to know how to manage a financial windfall?

- Are you trying to leave a legacy and want to know how you can pass more of your wealth along to your family and causes that are important to you—and less to the CRA?

History of Present Illness

As you think about your financial reality, where would you place yourself on these scales?

FINANCIAL DIS-EASE		FINANCIAL HEALTH
Worried	_____	Secure
Frightened	_____	At peace
Chaos	_____	Certainty
Despair	_____	Optimism

What strategies have been most instrumental in helping you get to where you are today? What mistakes have you learned to avoid?

Past Financial History

Just as common illnesses threaten health, common financial disorders threaten wealth. Here are some of the most common causes of *financial dis-ease*.

Pathologic Spending/Overspending. Think of spending like cardiovascular disease, which creates situations in which the demand for resources exceeds the supply.

Approximately 1.8 million (5%) of Canadians suffer from an addiction to shopping. Sometimes referred to as "shopaholism," out-of-control shopping can have the same devastating consequences as any other addiction. Physicians can also succumb to gambling addiction.

While the origin of addictive behaviors such as compulsive shopping, eating, and gambling remains uncertain, it's easy to understand why recovery is so difficult. The behaviors cause the release of endorphins and dopamine, which stimulate opiate receptor sites. In short, it feels good in the moment.

Pathologic Saving. The inability to spend, also called hoarding, can be as debilitating as overspending. This, too, is a condition that may require professional help.

Unmanaged Taxes. Think of taxes as a chronic malignancy that, left unchecked, erodes wealth. There is a simple cure; however, with proactive wealth-management strategies, you can build wealth while paying your legally owed taxes.

Financial Parasites and Pathogens. There is no shortage of people who want to prey on the "rich doctors." Physicians most vulnerable to this have what Dr. Harriet Braiker calls the "disease to please." She says that people who suffer from this disorder want to make people around them happy. They want to avoid conflict. It's much easier to give in to someone who wants something from you than to say no to family members or people from your place of worship.

Money Shame. Many physicians feel unworthy of wealth. They struggle with money shame. Some physicians have shame about their childhood poverty; others have shame about their childhood wealth. Some physicians experience shame about the poor financial choices they made in the past. Paradoxically, shame keeps them from seeking the help they need.

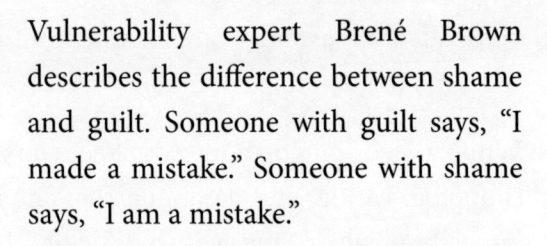

Vulnerability expert Brené Brown describes the difference between shame and guilt. Someone with guilt says, "I made a mistake." Someone with shame says, "I am a mistake."

What's the difference between the group of people who experience guilt and others who experience shame? The kinds of mistakes they make? The consequences of their mistakes? No! There's only one difference. The people living with guilt instead of shame make one simple choice: They decide they are worthy.

In other words, shame is an inside job.

Review of Systems

What are your current financial obligations? What financial obligations will you encounter in the next five years? Ten years? Twenty years?

How much joy do you derive from the items and experiences that you purchase?

How to Identify Addictive Spending

Here are some signs of compulsive shopping or gambling:

- Shopping to medicate emotional pain like sadness, anger, or loneliness
- Feeling a rush of euphoria after a purchase
- Hiding purchases or bills
- Lying about the true cost of items
- Juggling accounts to accommodate spending
- Feeling shame, guilt, or embarrassment about spending habits
- Experiencing strained relationships

If you recognize addictive shopping behavior in a loved one or even yourself, seek professional help. This is not a do-it-yourself job.

What is your greatest fear related to money?

Does your spending reflect your values?

Do you leverage your money to buy time by hiring others to do things you can delegate?

How well have your parents prepared for their golden years?

Does Money Buy Happiness?

Daniel Gilbert, author of *Stumbling on Happiness*, says, "Money is an opportunity that people routinely squander because the things they think will make them happy often don't."

In an article published in the *Journal of Consumer Psychology* entitled, "If money doesn't make you happy, then you probably aren't spending it right," Gilbert and his colleagues suggest the following:

- **Buy more experiences and fewer things.** You can anticipate and remember an experience, so you appreciate them longer.

- **Spend money to help others instead of yourself.** As Winston Churchill said, "We make a living by what we get. We make a life by what we give."

- **Buy many small pleasures instead of few big ones.** The authors say, "As long as money is limited by its failure to grow on trees, we may be better off devoting our finite financial resources to purchasing frequent doses of lovely things rather than infrequent doses of lovelier things."

- **Pay now, consume later.** Research shows that delaying gratification leads to greater satisfaction and happiness.

- **See the bad with the good.** Everything you buy requires time and attention. Purchases, like medical interventions, have potential risks along with the benefits.
- **Stop the comparison shopping.** You can help yourself avoid buyer's regret.
- **Ask your friends.** Research suggests that the best way to predict how much we will enjoy an experience is to see how much someone else enjoyed it.

Habits

Your financial habits shape your financial destiny. Here are the three habits that make a huge difference:

- Your propensity to spend and save
- The way in which you respond to financial pain
- How you make your financial choices.

Are You a Spender or a Saver? Some people are born "spenders" and others are born "savers." The evolving fields of behavioral finance and neuroeconomics suggest that each of us has a hard-wired biological spending-saving set point.

While biology is not destiny, it takes self-discipline for spenders to save—and for savers to spend. This requires active, disciplined effort, like holding a beach ball under water. Discipline is like a muscle and gets fatigued with prolonged use.

Unbalanced spending leads to financial troubles, and unbalanced saving leads to regrets.

The propensity to spend or save impacts your ability to meet your monthly expenses.

More importantly, it impacts your ability to build wealth. We physicians already get a late start on saving. The earlier you begin saving, the less you will have to save to achieve your financial goals. This means that the physician who starts saving and investing right out of training will do better.

We're also human. After so many years of deprivation, it's easy to quickly grow into, and even outspend, any salary. As some often suggest as a prudent solution: "Spend like you did as a resident."

Here are the most common causes of unhealthy spending:

- **Spending as a stress-management tool.** Stress is a specialized pain signal that alerts you to the fact that you are experiencing scarcity; you don't have enough of something. Retail therapy is a highly effective way to medicate the pain of stress in the moment. Shopping triggers the release of dopamine. You immediately feel better just as you would if you ate a pint of ice cream or devoured some chocolate chip cookies. The problem is that all of these temporary solutions ultimately do more harm than good. Here's a healthier response to stress. Ask yourself, "What do I need more of? Human connection? Support? Recognition?" Then get it!

- **Spending to solve nonfinancial problems.** Are you feeling guilty about not spending more time with your partner or missing your kids' piano recital? Sometimes physicians try to "purchase" their way out of unpleasant feelings like guilt. (Or the partners do it themselves!) Here's a healthier response: offer an apology and be there next time.

- **Unwillingness to say no.** How do you handle requests for loans and donations? Some physicians lend more than they can afford to lose.

What Is Your Pain Personality?

Pain—whether physical, emotional, or financial—is like the warning light on the car dashboard. It's a call to action.

Just as each of us has a style of dressing, similarly, each of us has a style of addressing pain signals. We noticed five patterns, which we call the pain personalities™: The Strong Stoic, The Worried Well, The Ostrich, The Victim, and The Ideal.

This pain personality usually predicts a person's response to physical, emotional, and financial pain.

This pain personality may be shaped in childhood and is largely unalterable.

Knowing your personality is like knowing your tennis swing. If you know your natural serve pulls to the right, you make adjustments to get the ball where you want it to go. Similarly, once you know your pain personality, you can adjust your response to achieve financial health most effectively.

The Strong Stoic

A sturdy Scandinavian patient once said, "You needed to be near death's door before Mother called the doctor. Sure, money was tight. I think the real reason we didn't go to the doctor was pride. Although Mother never said it, we knew that being healthy and being tough were sources of pride. Illness was a shameful condition that we tried to hide." Strong stoics may try to manage their own finances as a matter of pride.

The Worried Well

Do you know anyone who has a solid financial base, but is still haunted by the irrational fear of becoming homeless? Another name for this person is the "financial hypochondriac." These are intelligent people who think they are doomed to a life of poverty every time the market is down rather than up.

The Ostrich

We all need a healthy dose of denial to get on with our days. However, denial can go overboard and threaten financial health. The Ostrich who buries his head in the sand often has unopened portfolio statements and overlooked financial obligations.

The Victim

Some people see themselves as victims of external circumstances. "Look at what's happening to my taxes!" or "What am I supposed to do about the ACA? I may as well just shut down my practice!" They think they're powerless to change their reality. A Victim's words express a desire to achieve financial health, but their actions say something quite different.

The Ideal

This is the person who is engaged, makes proactive choices, and has a well-calibrated intuition.

Which one are you? Conflicting pain personalities can help explain money conflicts. Imagine a Strong Stoic married to a Worried Well!

How Do You Make Financial Choices?

Dr. Vicki once had a patient with multiple personality disorder. She described an experience captured in the movie *Inside Out*. A committee of people live in her head, and in any one moment, one committee member is in the driver's seat guiding her actions. In the movie, the characters include Joy, Sadness, Disgust, Anger, and Fear.

Imagine having a committee in your head making your financial choices. Here are some common committee members:

- **The Responsible Steward:** This person makes thoughtful, considered plans. This is who you want making most of your decisions.

- **The Competitor:** In the movie Wall Street, Gordon Gekko explains to his protégé, "It's not about the money. It's about the game." The Competitor is the committee member who wants to prove that he or she is the winner. His motto might be, "He who dies with the most toys wins." They don't want to just keep up with the Joneses; they want to beat the Joneses.

- **The Bon Vivant:** This is the committee member who wants to live it up today because she doesn't know what tomorrow might bring. It's like the athlete who throws million-dollar parties. This is the Alfred E. Neuman "What, me worry?" person.

- **The Child:** This is the committee member who wants what he wants when he wants it. Or else.

- **The Worrier:** This is the committee member who is always worried that homelessness and hunger are right around the corner.

- **The Greed Monster:** This committee member wants to collect more money simply to have more money.

- **The People-Pleaser:** This committee member wants everyone to be happy. This person may give money to others to minimize conflicts.

Clearly, you are best served when the Responsible Steward is making your financial choices. However, also be aware that at any given moment, any committee member could be in the driver's seat.

Who makes most of your spending choices? Your investing choices?

Family History

As children we learned lessons about money. We have a natural inclination to re-create our childhood financial reality.

If we grew up in scarcity, we tend to create scarcity by outspending our incomes. This explains why many lottery winners and professional athletes end up broke.

If we grew up with a mind-set of abundance, we tend to create abundance in our adult lives.

Consider the lessons your parents taught you about money.

Your Defining Money Story

Think about your earliest memory about money. What was it?

Think about a defining money moment in your life in which you understood the power of money to impact your life choice.

Mike remembers being about four and asking his father to buy a toy sheriff kit as they were paying for items at the store. His dad said, "Son, I can't afford it. You'll have to make your own money."

Mike got home, took out construction paper and a green crayon, and drew some counterfeit dollar bills. He took this to his father. They went back to the store where the shop owner accepted this "money" for the toy.

Janet remembers a university episode that still stings. Nine friends needed one more person to get a table at a new restaurant. They called her and invited her to join them. She was too ashamed to tell them that she could not afford to go out to dinner, so she made an excuse about needing to study. Then her friends got angry with her, called her selfish, and told her she was not a good friend; she let nine people down.

Jack found himself worrying about money in 2008. He was afraid he might be homeless sometime soon. However, Jack had over $10 million in assets when the market was at its lowest point. However, his family was, in fact, homeless during the Great Depression. He was experiencing "financial PTSD"—reliving a childhood financial trauma.

If you find yourself behaving irrationally about money, consider whether this reminds you of something you experienced in the past.

What Is Your Mind-set about Money?

When you think about money, what thoughts and phrases pop into your head?

Mind-set #1: Money is good. On one episode of Shark Tank, the Sharks talked about how much they loved everything about money—the feel of it and the scent of it. It's hard to imagine a physician saying those words out loud.

Mind-set #2: Money is bad, dirty, or evil. For most physicians there is something "dirty" about money. Discussing it feels less than professional. During medical school and residency, money was not mentioned. For many Canadian doctors, talking about money in the same sentence as discussing health care seems quite incongruent.

Mind-set #3: Money is neither bad nor good; it's simply a tool. Money serves a simple purpose: it facilitates the exchange of value. And value, like beauty, is in the eye of the beholder.

You may have spoken with an aging physician who practiced during the Great Depression. Did he accept chickens as compensation for his services?

In other words, money, like a hammer, is not inherently good or bad. It's simply a tool. You decide whether you will use the right tool for the right job; it is the way that money can be used for good or for bad.

What is your current mind-set about money? What would you like it to be?

What Do You Tell Yourself about Money?

Your parents communicated messages to you about the meaning of money and how money is used. You have beliefs about the role of money and the goal of building wealth.

Here are some word tracks that physicians say that impact their ability to build wealth.

- "I deserve nice things." You and your family made sacrifices to answer this call to medical service. When physicians finally start earning their six-figure incomes, they feel that it's time to splurge.
- "There will always be more than enough money." This physician fails to plan, trusting that there will be a bright financial future. Without a plan, money tends to wander off.
- "You invested in a marijuana farm with a 200 percent return? Count me in!" Physicians can follow trusted colleagues into marginal investments called dumb doctor deals (DDDs).
- "Look at me!" This physician wants to maintain the appearance of success at the cost of building true wealth.
- "Sure, I trust you." Physicians' trusting nature makes them easy targets for embezzlement, fraud, and ploys.
- "I'm embarrassed." Many physicians avoid seeking the help they need because they are embarrassed about financial mistakes in their past.
- "Mother Teresa took a vow of poverty; I should too." This physician believes that service and wealth are mutually exclusive.

No Silver Spoons

Do wealthy physicians inherit their wealth? Based on conversations with colleagues, we would estimate that the majority of wealthy physicians grew up in middle-class families. Most started saving early and got jobs when they were teenagers.

They attribute their success to hard work and self-discipline.

What Are You Teaching Your Children about Money?

What are you teaching your children about the meaning of money, the value of money, and how to make wise financial choices? What do they hear and observe as they watch you manage money?

Do your kids experience the financial consequences of their actions? If they lose their smartphone, do they contribute to replace it?

Do they get an allowance? Do you show them how to allocate the money between saving, giving to the less fortunate, and spending?

What is the right age to start talking to your children about money? How much do you disclose about your own personal net worth? Inheritance discussions? Intergenerational wealth transfer talks?

NOTES

NOTES

NOTES

3 YOUR OBJECTIVE FINANCIAL PICTURE

You have just gone through the exercise of learning more about your subjective money story.

Now let's look at your objective financial reality.

Your Financial Vital Signs

Imagine trying to manage patients without vital signs! Vital signs are vital. And financial vital signs help you manage your money and track your financial health.

Your Net Worth

Net worth is traditionally defined as your total assets minus your total liabilities. But here's the big question: How do you define an asset and a liability?

The traditional definition of an asset is something that you own, which, if sold, would put money in your bank account.

Medscape's 2018 Physicians' Debt and Net Worth report offered the survey results from about 20,000 physicians. Asset types included money in bank accounts, investments, retirement accounts, home equity, the value of cars, the value of jewelry, and other valuable items. Liabilities included debts such as money owed on mortgages, car loans, credit card debt, school loans, home equity loans, and the like. While the reports vary, approximately 50 percent of physicians report net worth of less than $1 million.

Net worth offers a static picture of your investments at any one point in time. It's a scorecard that shows how well you're accumulating things of value. Sometimes you buy things that enhance the quality of your life, like a nice set of golf clubs. Other times you make investments with the intention of selling at a higher price than you paid.

Do you know your own personal net worth as of today? If you don't, we highly recommend that you spend some time to figure it out ASAP. There are many simple spreadsheets available online or from your financial advisors, if you need a template.

Investments, Assets, and Liabilities. Here's the big question: Why do you care about net worth?

Your net worth is a financial vital sign with practical value; it offers a great prognostic indicator of the quality of your life in retirement. You can project the dynamic picture of money flowing in and out of your household each month.

You may prefer not to have to sell your home or your art collection to pay your monthly expenses. While there are ways to access the equity in your home through lines of credit or reverse mortgages, you want to avoid painting yourself into a financial corner.

When you are under financial stress and sell assets to get your hands on quick cash, you sell at a price that might be a fraction of the true value you could get if you had time to be patient

Do you have an emergency fund or a rainy day fund? If not, you may want to start one. The bigger question is, how large should it be, which is a widely variable number with many inputs to consider.

You're building wealth to avoid financial stresses! That's the whole point. You want to be in a situation of knowing with certainty that you will be able to meet your monthly expenses for life.

So for purposes of our conversation, let's define an asset as something that puts money in your pocket. Your practice might be an asset. So are income-producing investments, royalties from your intellectual property, and rent from rental property with a positive cash flow.

Let's define a liability as something that takes money out of your pocket. That could include your student loans, your mortgage, and lease payments on medical equipment. So is your car, unless you're an Uber driver.

Let's define an investment as something you buy with the intention of making money by selling it at a higher price than you paid or by generating dividends. Your home is an investment that, by these definitions, is a liability until the day you sell it.

As a wise investment advisor once said, most things that you own (or invest in) can be divided into four main categories, and it makes sense for us to think of our assets in this way: growth, income, stability, or speculation. In the future, as you make new investments, try to place items in these categories. It really makes you think about your goals.

Your Credit Score

YYour credit score might contribute to your ability to build wealth. Here are the top three benefits of good credit scores:

- Good credit scores make it easier to secure credit to buy a house, build your practice, or make investments.
- Good credit scores lower the cost of borrowed money. You might be able to negotiate lower interest rates on loans.
- Good credit scores might help you get better insurance rates.

Physicians as a group are creditworthy. In fact, many financial institutions offer special "doctor loans" for health care professionals in early stages of training. Build and protect your credit score.

Your Current Financial I's and O's: How Money Flows In and Out of Your Household

Your credit score might contribute to your ability to build wealth. Here are the top three benefits of good credit scores:

- Good credit scores make it easier to secure credit to buy a house, build your practice, or make investments.
- Good credit scores lower the cost of borrowed money. You might be able to negotiate lower interest rates on loans.
- Good credit scores might help you get better insurance rates.

Physicians as a group are creditworthy. In fact, many financial institutions offer special "doctor loans" for health care professionals in early stages of training. Build and protect your credit score

Income: Think After-Tax Dollars

As you well know, it's not what you make that's important; it's what you bring home. Taxes are your biggest expense. We have spoken with physicians whose retirement plans vanished as they faced unexpected tax bills.

Income from different sources might be taxed at different rates:

Earned income (Active income): You exchange your time and/or expertise for money. This form of income is typically taxed at the highest rate. Salaries and sales profits are examples.

Passive income: You make money—usually recurrent income—from your investments. This might include the rent you collect when you buy rental property or royalties from intellectual property you create. Other examples are interest income, dividends, and capital gains. In general, passive income is typically taxed at the lowest rate.

As of 2018, the government of Canada introduced new rules for passive income that could affect your tax position. Check with your accountant to see what specifically applies to your situation.

Your Financial I's and O's in Retirement

Let's describe retirement as the time in which you do not need earned income to pay your bills. This gives you the freedom to spend your days any way you wish, whether it's getting together with grandkids, traveling, or continuing to see patients.

What Is Your Retirement Dream? Imagine you had a magic wand, and any retirement lifestyle dream could come true. What would that dream be? Think in terms of three levels of living:

- The Minimum Acceptable Retirement
- The Living Big Retirement
- The Shooting for the Stars Retirement

For example, your minimum acceptable retirement might include a two-week vacation. In your living big retirement, you take your whole family on a two-week vacation to a tropical island. In your shooting for the stars dreaming big retirement, you own the island.

How much do you expect you will need on a monthly basis—in after-tax dollars—to comfortably fund your retirement lifestyle at these levels?

What Is True Financial Freedom?

Financial freedom is the state in which you know with certainty that you will never outlive your money. One big unknown is how long will you live after you retire.

Some people plan to put aside enough to pay their expected bills during their projected life-spans. Let's say Dr. Jones wants to spend $100K a year in retirement, and his projected life-span is twenty years. Just for sake of argument, let's also say he lives in an inflation-free world and has cash saved in his mattress. That means he would need to have saved $2 million that he expects to support his retirement for life. What happens, though, if he lives for twenty-five years?

Now compare him to Dr. Smith who made investments in real estate during his working years. Now the rents that he collects can finance his retirement; he does not need to sell his assets. Dr. Smith is set no matter how long he lives.

Clearly, these are simplified cartoon-like scenarios to illustrate a simple point.

Let's define **true financial freedom** as the situation in which your investments become like the goose that keeps laying the golden eggs. With this plan, you will never outlive your money, and you will have a legacy to pass on to the next generations

What Is Your Number?

Most people worry about outliving their money. Many physicians want to know, "What is my number? How big does my portfolio or my net worth need to be to fund my retirement?" The answer of course is, "It depends." What revenue streams will replace earned income in your retirement?

Are You on Track?

Are you on track to achieve your financial goals? Your current financial picture represents the results of the choices you have made up to this moment. If you do not know where you are right now, find out!

Have you taken advantage of the tax-sheltered investment vehicles available to you (such as RRSP, TFSA, RESP)?

If you are not where you would like to be, you are not alone. Starting today you can make different choices that lead to a different financial outcome.

If you want a different result, it means making changes. As you well know, changing financial habits is no easier than quitting smoking or losing weight.

	Can you meet your monthly expenses today?	Can you meet your monthly expenses if your earned income ended today?	Can you meet your monthly expenses for life?
Yes	Rich	Wealthy	Financially Free
No	In Debt	Vulnerable	Dependent
To Get to Yes	Spend Less Than You Earn	Create Streams of Passive and Investment Income	Accumulate Enough to Live off the Income Your Assets Generate

What Is the Path to Financial Freedom?

Here is your path to financial freedom.

Step #1: Be grateful for what you have.

Step #2: Budget your way to becoming rich by spending less than you earn.

Step #3: Invest your way to becoming wealthy by setting aside earned income to purchase investments that will generate passive income.

In Part II you will get some ideas about how to optimize your earning potential. In Part III you will see how to put your money to work making money!

PART II

GENERATING MORE EARNED INCOME

4 THE NEW THRIVING MEDICAL PRACTICE: WORKING SMARTER—NOT HARDER

Rodger is a physician in acute financial pain. Last year he saw a 15 percent decrease in his income when his major income-producing investments lost significant value. This year he will most likely bring home less than he did last year.

Sure, he makes almost a healthy income. Still, making less hurts!

He's pushing himself to work harder and longer to stop the financial bleeding. At his age, he hoped to be cutting back on his hours and ER call.

Rodger considers his choices. Pull the kids out of private school? Contribute less to his retirement fund? Scale back or even cancel the family vacation?

To make sure he meets his monthly practice expenses, he saw his banker and took out a line of credit.

Rodger remembers a time a decade ago when he actually looked forward to arriving at his practice. Today that joy is all but forgotten.

We hear stories like this one every day.

Here's the problem: The status quo—the way you've always done things—offers limited utility in getting ahead. Working harder and faster will only take you so far.

It's time to step off the hamster wheel and do things in a different way.

Your Income

IIn your current practice setting, the revenue you generate for yourself or for your employer likely correlates with

- Your clinical activities,
- The schedule of benefits negotiated fees, and
- The number of hours you work and number of patients you see.

Today's Practice Reality

Some of your professional activities bring you more personal, professional, and financial rewards than others. What if you spent more time in your "sweet spot" where your purpose, passion, and profitability meet?

You don't have to choose between running a profitable practice or dedicating yourself to service. You can have both.

Further, you ignore the money of medicine at your peril. We know a colleague dipping into her RRSPs to meet her payroll. Her constant financial concerns drain her energy.

Times Are Changing

The formula for practice success was simpler when students began their medical careers thirty years ago. One mentor advised, "Take good care of patients, and everything else will take care of itself."

Our colleagues and we believed that admission to medical school carried an implied promise of meaningful work, high incomes, and financial security.

Then again, it was a different technological time. Cell phones were about the size of a shoe, no computer at home, and the belief that a tweet was the sound birds made.

How things have changed!

Google, Facebook, and patients' access to global health care resources fundamentally changed the landscape of health care delivery and the doctor-patient relationship. In the language of real estate, we are shifting from a seller's market to a buyer's market. Patients are increasingly in the driver's seat directing health care choices.

In the post-Google world, taking good care of patients is necessary but no longer sufficient to build a thriving practice. Health care providers face classic business challenges:

- How do you attract and retain patients?
- How do you deal with competition?
- How do you hold down costs?
- How do you maintain and increase your revenue by working smarter and not harder?

Today the economic pressures underscore the importance of attending to the business side of your practice. As you will see, developing a healthier relationship with money may be a key element of your practice success.

The Trends

Here are some of the trends we have seen since the inception of Medicare in Canada in 1966, and its full implementation in all provinces by 1972:

Evolution of the doctor-patient relationship. The evolution of the relationship between doctor and patient very much parallels the relationship between a parent and a child.

In the Father Knows Best era, physicians did things to and for patients. They believed they were in a better position than the patient to make medical choices. This is like parenting a young child.

The sixties brought a change in the patient's status. The doctrine of informed consent said that patients had the right to make their own informed medical choices. The doctor's job was to lay out the risks and benefits of each alternative direction, and the patient would choose. This shift was like giving the car keys to teenagers.

Today's doctor-patient relationship looks more like an adult-adult collaboration.

Access to information. Historically physicians were the gatekeepers of medical information. It was difficult for patients to physically gain access to medical information, and when they got their hands on the clinical studies, they were largely incomprehensible to lay readers.

Today, patients go online to determine where and when they seek care. They read physician reviews and schedule appointments.

Medical information is now ubiquitous. However, patients still need a trusted advisor addressing the all-important question, "What does this information mean for ME?"

Transparency about costs. Go to your provincial ministry of health website and see that patients can learn what each billing code pays. For noncovered services, such as cosmetic procedures, patients can shop online and comparison shop.

Do You Run a Small Business?

When asked this question, most physicians say, "No, I run a medical practice," or "No, I'm an employee."

Yet, thriving physicians know they are running small businesses.

Yes, it's a specialized, hybrid business venture, but the process of building a successful business transcends the details of who is selling what to whom.

This idea may make you feel uncomfortable. What did you learn in your training about managing the business side of medicine? Who taught you how to negotiate contracts or leases, hire or fire employees or cut down on expenses? If you are like most physicians, the answer to most of these questions, is "nobody."

How Do Medical Practices and Small Businesses Compare?

Here are some qualities you share with entrepreneurs running small businesses:

- You both generate revenue.

- You both manage employees.

- You both have expenses.

- You both pay taxes.

- You both use the revenue you generate to provide for your families.

The metrics by which you measure success separate you from a small business owner.

- Small businesses win by optimizing profits. It's fundamentally about Financial outcomes.

- Medical practices win by optimizing the quality of medical care. It's fundamentally about clinical outcomes.

The formal training and skills that support success are different.

- You have formal training to perform diagnostic and therapeutic interventions.

- Small business owners generally have training in sales, marketing, and finance.

The relationship with the stakeholders is different.

- In small businesses, the consumer generally makes purchasing choices, writes the check, and uses the product or service. Think about purchasing a car, booking a vacation, or hiring someone to do yard work.

- In your practice, you manage complex triangulated relationships. The patient is the direct beneficiary of your services, yet their provincial insurance pays most or all of your fees. Patients' purchasing choices are generally made by the time they arrive at your office. If they are there, chances are good they will become your patient.

Why Do Business Strategies Matter to You?

Today, patients are behaving more like consumers.

- Patients are driving more health care choices. They have access to medical information. They can possibly even initiate diagnostic and therapeutic interventions without physicians. They have more financial skin in the game, and there is greater transparency about pricing.
- Patients increasingly drive referrals, either directly or indirectly. They choose where and when they seek medical services in much the same way you book air travel: on the basis of cost and convenience and the overall experience. Patients have access to a global health care market. Thousands will go overseas for medical care.

When patients behave more like consumers, you optimize your chances of success by embracing sound business practices.

What Are the Basic Rules in the World of Business?

In business, consumers exchange their money for the value they seek. They pay for transformations.

Value, like beauty, is in the eye of the beholder. Successful brands, from Apple to Nordstrom to Taylor Swift, regularly interact with their customers and fans to understand what's important to them.

Howard Putnam, the CEO of Southwest Airlines, said that they did not just guess at what their customer thought; they regularly interviewed their passengers, who were captive audiences in flight. When was the last time you asked your patients to complete a survey for you?

What do these rules mean for you? Historically, we physicians have conducted ourselves as the experts meeting our patients' medical needs.

Thriving physicians know that their incomes depend on their ability to understand why and when patients seek medical care, what's important to them, and how to inspire them to take action.

Do You Need Sales and Marketing Skills?

Your practice success is a direct result of your ability to persuade best-fit patients, your team members, and referring physicians to take action. Does this mean that you need marketing and sales skills? The short answer is yes.

Your ability to build rapport and influence others is a leadership skill that will serve you well at work, at home, and at play.

Physicians' Old Beliefs about Marketing and Selling

Most of us, when we entered medical school, believed, "Doctors shouldn't sell; it's unprofessional." Further, we believed we didn't have to sell. If we just took good care of patients, our practices would grow.

New Beliefs about Marketing and Selling

Yet we made peace with sales and marketing. We reframed marketing as the process of engaging someone in a conversation;

we reframed selling as the process of inspiring someone to take action. The action may be as simple as eating better, exercising more, or taking medications as prescribed.

You market and sell every day. You market when you grab the attention of your kids, join a social media conversation, or get an email returned. You sell when you persuade your kids to practice the piano, help a colleague see things your way, or get your food prepared as you want it at a restaurant.

Every time you have an informed consent conversation, you are selling. You lay out the risks and benefits of several possible action plans and ask patients to choose. This is a respectful, professional, non-sales-type approach to selling, and we wish more salespeople adopted this model.

Don't Confuse Marketing and Advertising

Marketing is different than advertising. Advertising says with words and actions, "Let me tell you all about me." Marketing says with words and actions, "Let's talk about you."

Today, in the US and around the world, you see physicians advertise on radio, TV, and billboards. I [Dr. Varenbut] just flew home from a trip and noticed the pages in the airline magazine about top doctors in America. These are advertisements—and expensive ads at that!

Even in Canada, you now see physicians marketing their services online, through social media platforms, and in print journals.

Compare that to the huge investment the Mayo Clinic made to develop and grow their patient education portal. This marketing investment positions them as trusted experts. They see the return on the investment as patients seek care at the Mayo Clinic.

Canadian patients have also started exploring options for care outside the country and often ask about clinics and hospitals they were exposed to via various marketing campaigns.

Marketing is a better choice for most practices than advertising. Marketing positions you as an expert. Physicians are educators; the word doctor comes from the Latin root for teacher. In that sense, you can engage patients by delivering educational marketing materials that they want to receive. A marketing campaign might include shooting videos with answers to your patients' most frequently asked questions.

A strong word of caution is to make sure to check with your provincial regulators with respect to specific guidelines on marketing, advertising, and testimonials. Many regulatory bodies have very strong positions on these subjects.

How Sales and Marketing Skills Impact Your Income

Here are three ways your ability to engage and persuade others can increase your income:

1. You attract more of your best-fit patients. Your ability to get noticed on social media, build relationships with more referring physicians, or offer your patients reasons to talk about you with their friends all have a direct impact on your bottom line.

2. You increase patient compliance. You enjoy many rewards for persuading more patients to take their medication as prescribed, adopt healthy lifestyle habits, or follow up as recommended. Better medical outcomes help you attract more patients. Better outcomes may also translate to higher income as patients are more likely to seek your care.

3. You build and lead effective teams. Your staff can help you create the experience that will attract more patients, cut costs, or deliver more value.

You will find amazing things happen as you enhance your powers of persuasion. Welcome to the world of sales!

Are You Ready for Money to Enter the Doctor-Patient Relationship?

If you are a baby boomer or belong to generation X, you may have assiduously avoided conversations about money with your patients. If patients asked you about costs, you may have said, "Speak with the office manager about that."

The Rules Are Changing

Today, patients are behaving more like consumers. When you are a consumer, you expect to look at a price tag. You would not buy a house or a car without knowing how much you will pay.

Patients want to talk about medical costs. It can and should enter into the informed consent conversation.

For many, many years patients were essentially paying medical bills with Monopoly money. Now that they have more financial skin in the game, they are factoring costs into their medical choices. Thriving physicians proactively address medical costs.

Your ability to overcome your discomfort in discussing fees makes it easier for patients to make good choices. Asking something as simple as, "Can you afford your medication?" can feel uncomfortable for everyone! But it is critical information.

Business Success Principles

Here are some business success principles that can help you run a more profitable practice:

Success Principle #1: In the world of business, consumers exchange their money for the goods and services they value. A patient may not care about her A1C, but she does care about being there to see her grandchildren born. Your job is to clearly communicate to patients the value that you deliver framed in a way that's most meaningful to them.

Success Principle #2: Begin a conversation about value before you discuss fees.

Myths about Patients and Money

Myth: It's unprofessional to talk about money.
Reality: Money is a common language spoken by insurance companies, the government, patients, and health care professionals. Successful physicians overcome their discomfort.

Myth: It's unprofessional to offer cash services to patients.
Reality: Products and services can be a way to extend your impact and create the financial security that can help you reach out to the medically underserved.

Myth: Patients will not pay out of pocket for medical services.
Reality: Patients spend money on things they value (concierge services, massage, supplements, cigarettes). Your job is to get them to understand the value you deliver.

Predictable Barriers to Health Care Spending

Different patients respond very differently to the idea of spending out of pocket for health care services. Here's why.

Patients' beliefs. How did you react the first time you were charged by an airline for carry-on luggage? Shocked? We believed that carry-on luggage was free (and it was, for a long time).

Some patients hold the belief that all health care services should be free. A colleague asks, "How do I charge when my patients ask me for medical notes, repeat prescriptions over the phone, or telephone advice?" You will certainly have patients that fall in this category; however, many patients will pay for the things that they value. In the height of the great recession, many paid billions of dollars out of pocket on weight loss, anti-aging therapies, and nutritional supplements.

Your goal is to attract the patients who do understand your value and are willing to pay for it. They are out there!

Patients' priorities. Have you ever had patients who tell you they cannot afford medication, but find the funds to smoke two packs of cigarettes a day? Generally, spending reflects underlying values.

Patients' failure to see value. Businesses understand it's their job to understand what customers want and clearly lay out their value.

As a physician, you value medical outcomes; patients value personal outcomes. They don't care about their cholesterol level as much as they value the ability to see their grandkids get married. Further, patients consider the overall experience. They make choices about medical care in much the same way you make other decisions in life.

Patients' skepticism about self-claims. Sophisticated consumers have their guards up for hype. Your website banner saying "center of excellence" is not as compelling as a patient's video testimonial or before-and-after pictures (where allowed by provincial regulators).

Tips for Talking with Your Patients about Fees

This will likely only apply to discussions about noncovered medical services, such as cosmetic procedures.

Here are a few questions that you can pose to patients to frame conversations about medical costs:

- "What is the outcome you hope to achieve as a result of this medical intervention?"

- "Doing nothing is always an option. What is the cost to you of not taking action?"

Some patients will shop for the lowest price. Other patients happily pay more for service or an experience they value.

How Do Physicians Overcome the Professional and Ethical Barriers to Business Success?

The biggest barrier to your professional success may be a set of beliefs about what constitutes conduct becoming to a physician. There's an unstated belief that these elements of business success, like sales and marketing and stating your value, put you in the class of snake oil salespeople.

We are here to suggest that if you are truly committed to serving patients, you have a duty to let members of your community know how you improve patients' conditions. Getting your message out there is not simply a self-serving way to increase your wealth; it offers the opportunity to help the patients you are here to serve.

Further, your ability to build wealth allows you to leave a bigger legacy and serve in a bigger way.

You don't have to choose between running a profitable practice and dedicating yourself to service. You can have both.

Some Things Never Change

Practice building has always been and will always be about relationship building.

However, the way you connect with patients—and people who make referrals—is different today than it was thirty years ago.

You can build your practice with business strategies that maintain the highest level of professionalism.

Reinvention is the operative word. Reinvention will help you achieve practice success in these rapidly changing times. You can reinvent the way you generate patient referrals. You can shed old marketing beliefs that weigh you down and adopt new practices that work in today's health care environment.

NOTES

NOTES

NOTES

5 ARE YOU LEAVING MONEY ON THE EXAM TABLE?

Would you be surprised to learn that physicians regularly walk away from 30 percent or more of their income?

Different groups of physicians leave money on the table for different reasons. Here are some of the most common mistakes that physicians make.Failure to Negotiate Contracts

Failure to Negotiate Contracts

In Sheryl Sandberg's book, Lean In: Women, Work and the Will to Lead, she shares that she was a seasoned executive when Mark Zuckerberg invited her to join Facebook as the COO. She says she was inclined to accept the first offer he made.

When she discussed it with her husband, he told her the first offer is just the starting point of a negotiation. He recommended she make a counteroffer. She did and Zuckerberg came back to her with a much more lucrative proposal.

If Sandberg reached her level of professional success without knowing basic negotiation etiquette, how many physicians make the same mistake?

Whether you are signing a contract with an employer, a cost-sharing agreement with other physicians in your practice, a buy-sell agreement, or even a lease, run it by legal counsel. Terms of agreement are not carved in stone; you can advocate for your own best interests.

Further, acquire some basic negotiation skills. The ability to persuade others is a skill that will serve you with colleagues, patients, and family.

Failure to Collect What You're Owed for Clinical Services

Insurance Claims

Physicians in private practice walk away from a portion of their incomes when they do not follow up on rejected insurance claims. Many physicians also often forget to bill for services that they provided, or procedures they completed. Being diligent on the details of the allowable billing codes and keeping close track of your work makes simple sense.

What is your claim rejection rate? Outsourcing your medical billing or providing additional training for your staff could bring claim rejection rates close to zero.. This may be the fastest and easiest way to increase your cash flow.

Patient Copays

Many medical practices suffer with a systems problem: They do not have policies and procedures in place to collect the portion of the bill for which patients are responsible. Traditionally, collection rates for third-party services, block fees, and noncovered services are extremely low.

Here are some ways to avoid these losses:

- Create a transparent payment policy that you share and discuss with all patients.
- Accept credit card payments at your office.
- Build relationships with companies that offer lending for medical procedures. That way you get paid in full, and the financial risks are transferred to the lenders (for example, for expensive cosmetic procedures)

Failure to Negotiate Terms of Loans

You will most likely borrow money to make big and small purchases. The interest that you pay on a loan is not carved in stone.

Shop around for mortgages. Some banks will match lower interest rates. Call your credit card company and ask them to decrease the interest that you pay.

You are in the best position to negotiate if you have high credit scores.

Failure to Scrutinize Expenses

Do you know what your monthly expenses are? Take a look at all of the goods and services you purchase and ask these questions:

- What is this for?
- Do I need it?
- Can I reduce or eliminate it?
- Can I get a better price somewhere else

Failure to Minimize Your Taxes

Make sure that you are doing everything possible to claim all of your lawful deductions and minimize your tax burdens. You are best served by working with an accountant who has extensive experience with physicians like yourself. Further, you want to work with an expert who knows various options for minimizing your tax burdens.

Take Advantage of the Financial Benefits of Incorporating

Did you know that the right corporate structure may offer tax savings, as well as possible protection of your assets in the event of a lawsuit? The corporation has to be structured in the right way. Check with your team and make sure that you have chosen the practice structure that makes the most sense for you.

Being Penny-Wise and Pound-Foolish

You have heard the expression, "You have to spend money to make money." Sometimes the unwillingness to make investments in yourself can be the costliest income mistakes you will make.

Here are wise ways to spend money that will allow you to increase your income potential:

- **Education and training.** Invest to expand your clinical knowledge, financial literacy, or business skills.
- **Marketing. Avoid being the best-kept secret in town.** However, it's always important to keep track of your investment of time, energy, and money and measure the

outcome. You want to get a healthy return on your investment (ROI). Or as we say, "Keep your eye on the ROI."

- **Buy more time.** Yes, you can clean your house and mow your lawn. If you find activities like these relaxing, please indulge! However, when you hire people to take care of these activities, you buy time to optimize your revenue.

- **Hire experts.** The investment you make seeking expert advice will almost always put you in a better financial position.

- **Buy protection.** Do not skimp on insuring the assets that have the most value to you, including your income potential. It's not a fun or sexy way to spend money, but when you need it, you'll be glad you had it.

Failure to Harness the Power of Leverage

Archimedes said, "Give me a lever long enough and a fulcrum on which to place it, and I shall move the world."

What is leverage? Think of an Allen wrench inserted into a screw. You can put the long end or the short end of the wrench into the screw. If you put the short end in, you have a longer lever arm. This allows you to get more results from your efforts.

You leverage your staff to optimize your ability to generate revenue. Could you hire a partner, a nurse practitioner, or a physician's assistant to allow you to engage in more profitable activities?

You leverage borrowed money to make investments, whether it's new equipment or a practice makeover. Explore whether it makes more financial sense to own or to lease your office space, equipment, or car. Your accountant or financial advisor can offer their opinions.

In chapter 8, you will see that leveraging borrowed money is a habit of wealth.

Good Debt versus Bad Debt

Debt is simply borrowed money; it is inherently neither good nor evil. However, the use of the borrowed money distinguishes between good debt and bad debt.

Good debt leverages borrowed money to build wealth. Some examples of good debt include medical school loans, the right real estate investments, or a practice buy-in.

Bad debt is used to purchase a thing or an experience that will not increase in value. Some examples include a car, a European vacation, or a designer suit.

Embrace good debt; eschew bad debt.

Failure to Protect against Fraud and Embezzlement

Do you have checks and balances in place to help keep your employees honest? A colleague of Dr. Vicki's told her that she should have listened to her intuition about her "trusted office manager." She discovered that over the years, this person embezzled hundreds of thousands of dollars.

Here are some steps you can take to decrease the risk of theft at your office:

Hire the right people. Verify the information provided by the applicant. Call references. Conduct a criminal and credit check for all new employees. Create a written policy outlining your zero tolerance of fraud and have each employee sign it.

Use a lockbox for petty cash. Nearly half of all theft involves cash from copays or petty cash. Do what you can to keep honest people honest.

Divide financial duties. The person collecting the cash should be different than the person reconciling transactions.

Implement safe banking practices.

- Sign your own checks. Get rid of signature stamps. Restrict online banking access.
- Pay bills online.
- Get bank statements sent to your home.

Purchase business liability insurance that includes coverage for employee theft and embezzlement.

Bond all staff who process payments.

Purchase identity theft insurance. You may be able to purchase a rider with your home insurance policy.

Confirm that your office and personal insurance covers you for cybercrime. In this day and age, we hear of many stories of individuals and business that have fallen victim.

Know the warning signs. Worrisome employee behavior includes

- Spending habits that exceed salaries
- Refusal to take vacations or time off
- Missing receipts, invoices, or purchase orders
- Overdue notices from vendors
- Patient complaints about billing errors

- Unexplained shortages of petty cash
- Unusual patterns in bank deposit statements

Listen to your gut. If you are worried about an employee, don't dismiss the concern.

Your accountant may be a good resource if you suspect fraud or embezzlement.

NOTES

NOTES

NOTES

NOTES

6 TEN WAYS TO GENERATE MORE REVENUE

You made a significant investment to enjoy the privilege of caring for patients. You made sacrifices. You work long hours. Are you enjoying the financial fruits of your labour?

Strategies and tactics to optimize your revenue fall into one of three basic categories:

1. **Stop losing money. (This was the subject of the previous chapter.)**
2. **Tweak your current practice model.**
3. **Add additional income streams.**

In this chapter, you will see at least ten ways to put more money in your hands. We will begin with the plans that are easiest to implement and then move to more dramatic interventions.

Remember that your value transcends your ability to diagnose and treat individual patients. You can help many people in many different ways—and get paid for it.

As Paul Desmarais III of Power Financial Corporation recently said, "Innovation and technology applied to the healthcare industry will drive sustainability." We hope that Canadian physicians can continue to be the nidus of new products, services, and innovations that will undoubtedly create value for all.

1. Moonlight

Here are some revenue-generating activities you can fit into your existing schedule.

Serve as an expert in medical malpractice lawsuits.

Here are the three benefits of this work:

1. This work is well-compensated.

2. You can fit this work into your schedule.

3. Reviewing these cases can make you a better physician. When you see where care goes off track, it makes it easier to keep care on track.

Here are three reasons this work is not right for everyone:

1. The adversarial environment of a courtroom can be very draining.

2. You may need to make investments to build a successful legal consulting practice.

3. You can only perform these duties for a limited number of years after your retirement. Experts are asked to comment on the standard of care of a reasonably prudent physician practicing in the community at the time the care was delivered. Experts have the most credibility if they were practicing at the time of the untoward event.

Further, if you have been traumatized by the experience of defending yourself in a lawsuit, this may not be a good fit for you.

You could take locums positions, serve as medical director in medically supervised weight-loss programs, or get on staff at assisted living facilities. If you are in private practice, consider signing up for ER call in your medical specialty. You might take on shifts offering opinions as a telemedicine consultant or reviewing insurance claims. Other examples are physicians who added roles such as a hospitalist, surgical assistant, and nursing home attending staff.

2. Focus

Get very, very good at helping a specific kind of patient achieve a specific medical outcome.

Some physicians fear that narrowing their clinical scope will slow referrals. While this sounds counterintuitive, experience demonstrates that focus accelerates practice growth.

Here are a few examples:

The Shouldice Hospital in Canada performs one surgical procedure: the Shouldice repair of inguinal hernias. Their published 99 percent lifetime success rate for primary hernias attracts patients from all around the world.

A urologist focuses his practice on adult male circumcisions.

A GP-anesthetist focuses on providing sedation at outpatient endoscopy clinics.

An anesthetist practicing full-time in a chronic pain clinic provides interventional treatments.

A psychiatrist treats patients addicted to opiates in an outpatient opiate-substitution clinic.

A dentist takes delight in treating phobic patients who have not been in a dental chair for years.

You could focus on a specific procedure, a specific disease process, or a specific patient population.

Three things happen when you narrow your scope of practice. First, you get better medical results. Second, you can scrutinize every step of the care process for ways to enhance efficiencies and reduce costs. Third, you increase your chances of delivering the patient experience that will generate more referrals.

3. Leverage Staff

> All of your employees have value. They are on the front line, representing you! They have ideas that can create a better experience for your patients and colleagues. Survey them. Solicit their input. Express your gratitude for their dedication

In the traditional practice of medicine, you exchange your time for your fees. Your staff can help you optimize your fees in a number of ways.

If you want to increase your income, spend the bulk of your time in the most profitable activities. This means delegating activities that can be done by others.

Further, each of your employees can potentially serve as a profit center. Consider hiring PAs or nurse practitioners..

4. Add Clinical Services

Each additional service that you offer could potentially add a revenue stream to your practice. These could either be services you submit to provincial insurers or insurance companies or offer as a cash service.

Here are a few examples:

A physician added Botox and dermal filler cosmetic services.

A clinic added virtual care services to their patients.

A pediatrician added newborn circumcision services to a group of pediatricians

5. Change Practice Settings

Many physicians are making bold professional moves in response to the growing challenges in the health care system. Here are a few you may have considered.

Sell your private practice to another physician, group, or clinic. Some physicians have changed from private practice to employed positions within a variety of settings. Examples are academic positions, executive health clinics, corporate medical positions, and concierge medical groups.

Here are the advantages of employment:

- You have certainty about your salary.
- Your employer picks up many of your expenses, such as medical malpractice insurance, disability insurance, and health insurance.
- You get paid time off and are often paid continuing medical education benefits.
- Your contributions to your retirement plan may be matched by your employer.
- You focus on patient care; the business side of medicine is managed by administrators.
- You have a better chance at work-life balance.

Make a transition from employment to private practice. While the trends vary by medical specialty, practice setting, and province, some physicians are moving from employment to private practice. If you are considering this move, you have many important legal and financial issues to address that are beyond the scope of this book. It's important to get them right.

> ### Be Smart about Structuring the Purchase or Sale of a Medical Practice
>
> Buying and selling a medical practice is fraught with complexity. What is a fair purchase price? What are the tax consequences of the sale? We saw a deal in which both doctors lost 85 percent of the sale price to taxes! The way you structure the purchase or sale can radically impact the amount of money that stays in your hands. Check with experts to help you with both practice valuation and the structuring of the deal that has the most favorable tax consequences for you. You can read more about this topic in Part III.

Opt out of insurance plans. Some physicians are opting out of all insurance compensation and are transitioning to all cash practices. This is more often seen in cosmetic practices. If the ethics of cash practices are of concern to you, consider creating your own fund or a sliding scale, for patients who cannot afford to pay your fees.

6. Consider Moving

This sounds dramatic. Who would want to uproot their families? There may be personal reasons for moving, such as being closer to aging parents. In addition, there may be a strong financial reason.

Physician compensation may be shaped by geographic location. The cost of living in a geographic location shapes how far your dollars go. Take a look at real estate, and you will find that you can buy more house in one part of the country than another. The cost of goods and services might also vary.

Many physicians have tremendously improved their quality of life and financial stability and have reduced their overall level of stress by deciding to settle away from expensive metropolitan areas.

How much could you improve your financial condition and quality of life with a move? Check with your financial advisor or accountant to run the numbers.

7. Educate, Empower, and Entertain

You can generate income by leveraging what you know outside of the care of individual patients. Here are a few ways.

Educate. The word doctor comes from the Latin root meaning teacher. You can educate in a number of ways:

- Accept a faculty appointment at a medical, nursing, or dental school.

- Teach courses for colleagues or patients. One physician helps international medical graduates pass their qualifying examinations by teaching courses in his free time.

- Serve as a physician spokesperson. Speak as an invited expert at CME events locally and abroad (for example, offer CME content on a river cruise conference).

Empower. You could create programs and systems and host seminars to help patients get these desired results.

- Lose weight
- Look younger
- Sleep better
- Find love
- Keep their brains healthy
- Get fit
- Stop smoking
- Eat more healthfully
- Raise healthy kids
- Save money

Entertain. The public has a voracious appetite for stories from the world of medicine. You can get paid as a professional speaker, blogger, or author to tell these stories in a compelling way

8. Coach and Consult

Coaches and consultants help others achieve their desired outcomes. Here are a few ways you could generate additional income.

Create an online membership site. Charge your members—whether it's patients, colleagues, or family caregivers—a small monthly fee for gaining access to content that will help them

- Improve their quality of life,
- Learn about cutting-edge research,

- Share helpful products and services,
- Ask questions in a safe environment, or
- Provide a forum for peer-to-peer engagement.

As of this writing, there are over 250,000 medical apps, and many have been created by nonphysicians. Only 1,000 have been clinically validated. Perhaps you can improve on the quality of the existing apps?

Seek consulting opportunities. Many organizations are interested in the opinions and perspectives of physicians. Here are a few options:

- Pharmaceutical industry
- Medical device companies
- Businesses with health-related products
- Organizations developing health policy

Note: Please verify with your respective regulatory body as to the current regulations with respect to the specific activities mentioned here.

9. Assume Physician Leadership

The top earners in medical organizations are often not the physicians; they are the CEOs and administrators.

Have you ever seen yourself in a leadership position? Consider whether you would find career satisfaction by stepping into the role of a physician executive. Hospitals and clinics need strong leadership to assure that they remain profitable in these challenging times.

10. Start a Company

Some of the wealthiest physicians in the world accumulated assets through entrepreneurial efforts.

Do you have an idea for a medical app? Do you have a proprietary piece of intellectual property? Explore whether you want to build a company around this idea.

While you may not be an inventor, you can invest in start-ups—if you meet the criteria as an accredited investor.

In Canada, an accredited investor is defined by the provincial securities commissions throughout the country. While there are many items that can make up the definition of an accredited investor, for an individual, the definition typically includes a net worth of at least $1 million, or having income of at least $200,000 each year for the last two years (or $300,000 combined income if married).

Qualifying as an accredited investor also could open the doors for you to invest in a variety of alternative investments. These could include private equity investments, REITS (both private and public), and Angel investments. These might carry higher potential returns, but typically are also much higher risk. Please know your risk tolerance and act accordingly.

NACO (National Angel Capital Organization (www.nacocanada.com)) lists over twenty groups across the country that offer a great opportunity for exposure and participation in early-stage companies.

Where Can Accredited Investors Find Opportunities?

If you want to generate wealth by owning a share of a company, you may want to think like a Shark. Here's what the business-savvy Sharks know as they scrutinize investment opportunities:

- Look for disruptive technology: Find game-changing innovation. Assure that the intellectual property upon which the company is built is patent-protected.

- Look for a proven market: Make sure that the product or service solves a buyer's pressing problem. Further, gather evidence that the buyer has an incentive to make the purchase.

- Look for the right team: The process of bringing a product from the whiteboard to the marketplace requires a specialized skill set. Make sure that the team's principals know how to build businesses.

Owning a piece of a start-up company offers a way for you to make socially responsible investing choices that can support your own passions—while making the world a better place. There are also often opportunities for physicians to share their knowledge and expertise within new companies, creating added value prospects rather than just investing money.

Four Wealthiest Physicians in the United States

Some physicians measure their wealth in billions rather than millions. You do not get to this level of wealth through the practice of clinical medicine. All of the five wealthiest physicians in the United States launched entrepreneurial business ventures.

Patrick Soon-Shiong, MD ($11.5 billion net worth per Forbes as of June 2016): Dr. Soon-Shiong is the wealthiest physician in the US. After making a name for himself as a surgeon, he founded two drug companies, Abraxis and American Pharmaceutical Partners, which he sold for a combined $9.1 billion. He invented a cancer drug, Abraxane, which, after years of slow sales, is now a blockbuster thanks to its efficacy against pancreatic cancer. A member of the Buffett-Gates Giving Pledge, Dr. Soon-Shiong plans to give away at least half his fortune. He has donated $136 million to St. John's Health Center in Santa Monica, California. He owns a 4 percent stake in the Los Angeles Lakers basketball team.

Thomas Frist, Jr., MD ($8.2 billion net worth): Dr. Frist, a former Air Force flight surgeon, founded Hospital Corporation of America with his father in 1968 and took it public for the third time in 2011. He doesn't have an executive position at HCA, but his sons Thomas III and William are board members. His brother is Dr. William Frist, a transplant surgeon and former Majority Leader of the US Senate. The whole Frist family is deeply involved in local, national, and international philanthropy. The family is currently leading an effort to promote and improve health care in China.

Phillip Frost, MD ($3.9 billion net worth): Dr. Frost, who trained as a dermatologist, is a health care investor and executive. While practicing in Miami in the 1960s, he developed a disposable device to make biopsies easier. He partnered with Michael Jaharis to build a company around his invention. They sold Key Pharmaceuticals to Schering-Plough in 1986 for $835 million. He then became CEO of Ivax Corporation, which he sold to Teva in 2006 for $7.6 billion. The seventy-five-year-old Miami Beach resident serves on the Smithsonian Institution Board of Regents and the University of Miami Board of Trustees.

Gary Michelson, MD ($1.5 billion net worth): Dr. Michelson is an orthopedic and spinal surgeon-turned-inventor, investor, and philanthropist. Motivated by his grandmother's spinal deformity and frustrated with subpar surgical instruments, Dr. Michelson "tinkered" with medical device ideas for years in his garage. He holds more than 250 US patents for medical devices and procedures. In 2005, he became a billionaire when he reached a $1.35 billion settlement with Medtronic after years of litigation over his patents. Today, Dr. Michelson, a pet lover since boyhood, is focused on animal welfare. He started the Found Animals Foundation to help pet shelter overcrowding and has donated millions to research for animal care.

What's Right for You?

With all of these options, how do you identify what's right for you? Here are some steps:

Identify Your Sweet Spot

[Dr. Vicki's story] When my son was in Little League, he wanted to buy an expensive bat. I asked the clerk why this bat cost so much more than the others. He said, "It has a big sweet spot."

I asked, "What's a sweet spot?"

My son answered, "That's the part of the bat that hits home runs."

You have a professional sweet spot. When your day-to-day activities fall in your sweet spot, you hit more professional home runs. This is usually where purpose, passion, and profits meet.

The more you focus your time, attention, and resources on your sweet spot—whether it's seeing a certain kind of patient or performing a certain medical procedure—the greater satisfaction you will experience.

Ask Key Questions

Consider your answers to these questions to help you identify your sweet spot:

- How do I improve the condition of others?
- What are my gifts and passions?
- What is my value?

Ask people who know you well, "If I were on the cover of a magazine, what would the magazine be and what would the article be about?" or "If you could only call one person, under what condition would you call me?"

Acquire Key Skills

I have personally invested the equivalent of my medical school tuition acquiring the business skills I needed to support my professional goals. This has included seminars, courses, books, and a Master's degree in Business Administration.

What if you felt more comfortable with your ability to lead, market, sell, craft, and deliver services?

You invest in CME to assure you are offering your patients the best care possible. Does it not make sense to learn how to attract more of those patients to your practice, persuade colleagues, and help patients get optimal medical outcomes?

Does it also not make sense for you to dedicate more time and resources toward becoming more educated in financial aspects of your life?

Assemble Key Team Members

Even if you are temperamentally a lone wolf, success is a team effort. Make sure that you assemble a strong team and delegate tasks that do not fall in your sweet spot. We will also discuss our vision of the dream team for your financial well-being, later in the next sections.

Today, you can potentially help people across the globe, educate people whom you have never personally met, and deliver value in unique ways. This option offers unprecedented opportunities for you.

Income Is Just the Start

When you optimize your income, you put yourself in a position to build wealth more quickly. However, the way you manage your income will determine whether you join the group of wealthy physicians—or struggling physicians.

Would you like more ideas about how to get greater personal, professional, and financial rewards from your career? I invite you to go to
ThrivingDoctors.com and learn about more resources.

NOTES

NOTES

NOTES

PART III

PUTTING YOUR MONEY TO WORK AND GETTING BETTER RETURNS ON YOUR INVESTMENTS

We don't know about you, but given the choice of taking care of your patients or taking care of your money, we'd choose patient care. Every time.

At the very beginning of my [Dr. Varenbut's] medical career, saddled with significant medical school debt, I knew that someone needed to manage my money. I chose the path of delegation.

I ascribed to conservative, disciplined investing strategy. Work hard and save. Begin to invest early to take advantage of compound interest. Create a portfolio with a diverse collection of stocks and bonds. Minimize risk. Take advantage of the tax benefits of an RRSP.

I hired my own professional financial advisor. My advisor's stated goal was to help me beat the market. The firm advocated investing strategies and tactics that historically helped investors get the best return on their investments. I learned about the importance of keeping fees low by buying no-load mutual funds. I learned more about my own risk tolerance. I learned to avoid the mistakes I make when I follow my propensity to make emotional choices about money.

I had bought into the conventional beliefs about how to build wealth, literally and figuratively. This is similar to the advice from TV financial gurus.

At one point I asked my financial advisor about investing in real estate. He told me the stock market was a better choice. As I discussed this advice with a colleague, he said, "Of course your financial advisor doesn't want you pulling money out of your portfolio to make a real estate investment. He gets paid a percentage of your assets he manages, right?"

Then in 2008, I, like everyone else, wondered what to do. Stay in the market? Get out?

This is when I started speaking with more physicians about how they were managing their money. I learned that physicians who had built wealth saw the world of investing differently than struggling physicians. I saw trends emerge.

Wealthy physicians ask different questions than struggling physicians. They use different financial products. Their goal was not to beat the market. They simply wanted to make the smartest investments that minimized their risk and shielded them from losses.

Here's what's most important to wealthy physicians:

- How to avoid losses in a volatile market
- How to ethically and legally minimize tax burdens
- How to identify investments that offer big returns without taking big risks

I came to see that wealthy physicians use financial products and services I had never explored. This is like limiting your diagnostic and therapeutic tools to the options that you had ten or twenty years ago.

In Part I you got a handle on your financial health and developed a picture of where you want to be. In Part II you took away ideas about how to optimize your earned income.

Now, how do you build wealth? In Part III we will share with you the patterns we have discovered through years of conversations with colleagues about their money. You will learn some of the habits that separate thriving physicians from struggling physicians.

7 A NEW WEALTH-BUILDING APPROACH

There is no shortage of advice about how to build wealth. You can find information by reading books, listening to financial gurus, or swapping stories with your colleagues in the surgeons' lounge or doctors' dining room.

I would like to suggest that any given financial product or service is neither good nor bad; it's a tool. You want a financial plan that will help you and not harm you. And many physicians still feel the financial pain of 2008. They say, "I just want to make sure I don't lose what I have!"

Warren Buffett's rules of investing offer the financial service's version of our physician code: "First, do no harm."

Warren Buffett's Rules of Investing

Rule #1: Don't lose money.

Rule #2: Never forget Rule #1.

Sometimes the best answers to help you get to where you want to go defy conventional wisdom.

Please remain open to the possibility that a radically new wealth-building approach could transform your path to financial freedom. Just as there are new diagnostic and therapeutic tools to help you take better care of patients, there are new financial tools that can help you invest more like the wealthy do.

Wealth Building Is an Epic Task

You remember Homer's epic poem the Odyssey. The Greek hero Odysseus makes his ten-year journey home after the Trojan War. Along the way he confronts dangerous obstacles and foes that take the lives of all his men.

Likewise, your epic journey to wealth is fraught with danger. Just as Odysseus battled the lotus eaters, the cyclops, and the sea monster, you will confront forces that threaten your wealth.

We've already addressed a few: the economic impact of health care changes, theft, fraud, and embezzlement. Let's address others.

The Threats to Your Wealth

Taxes: What's your biggest expense? Your house? Your kids' college education? Indulging your love of cars?

The one thing that matters most when building wealth is how you manage taxes! Taxes are your biggest lifetime expense. Without proactive management, taxes will erode your wealth and the legacy you pass on to next generations.

Here are some truths that are very important to understand:

You will pay taxes every year of your life. As you consider your total tax burden, think in terms of three kinds of money:

- Taxed income (earned (active) or passive)

- Tax-deferred (money you take out of your RRSP and other retirement plans)

- Tax-free (death benefit and the cash value of a life insurance policy, disability and long-term care insurance—depending on how you pay for the policy)

You will pay taxes during your earning years.

Are You Paying More Than Your Fair Share of Taxes?

Would you benefit from a second tax opinion? Tax law is complex. While I'm certain your accountant is a nice person, there may be additional ways to legally and ethically lower your taxes through incorporation and other legal structures, claiming all deductions, or using the right investment products. We'll address this later on.

You will pay taxes during your retirement years. The way you structure your portfolio during your earning years determines how much of your money is yours in retirement—and how much belongs to the government.

You will pay taxes after you die. The way you structure your estate will have a direct impact on the percentage of your estate you pass on to generations to come. Work with a skilled estate planner.

You will pay taxes during your retirement years. The way you structure your portfolio during your earning years determines how much of your money is yours in retirement—and how much belongs to the government.

You will pay taxes after you die. The way you structure your estate will have a direct impact on the percentage of your estate you pass on to generations to come. Work with a skilled estate planner.

Your accountant sees his or her job as minimizing your taxes in any given year; to build wealth you want to minimize your lifetime tax burden.

While it hurts to pay taxes today, what do you think will happen to our taxes in the future? What will Canada's deficit be in the future, and how will this affect our tax rates?

Many physicians want their kids to graduate from college or university without debt. Our kids and many generations to come will begin their professional lives burdened with debt. How will we pay it back?

The best strategy is to access tax-free dollars in retirement.

> ### *Think about Giving*
>
> You can do well by doing good. The tax code is structured to provide financial incentives to those who take on behaviors that benefit all citizens, like creating jobs, providing housing, and supporting philanthropy. Structure your charitable donations in a way that makes your contributions go further, allows you to enjoy tax benefits during your life, and preserves your legacy after your death.

Judge Learned Hand said, "There is not even a patriotic duty to increase one's taxes. Over and over again the Courts have said that there is nothing sinister in so arranging affairs as to keep taxes as low as possible. Everyone does it, rich and poor alike and all do right, for nobody owes any public duty to pay more than the law demands."

Wealthy physicians say it's more important to minimize the impact of taxes when making investment decisions than it is to pursue the highest possible returns regardless of the

tax consequences. We typically think of earnings and investment returns in pre-tax dollars, rather than taking into account what we will actually keep. Make sure you don't fall into this trap.

Action Step: Understand that each financial choice has a tax consequence. When exploring investing options, ask, "How will this choice impact the taxes I pay this year and over my lifetime?"

Inflation: It might appear that the safest place for your money is in your mattress; however, that is the certain way to lose money. Your purchasing power gets eroded with each round of inflation. A rough guide to use is an inflation rate of 2 to 3 percent a year, which is where it has been in Canada in the past twenty years. This may, of course, change in the future.

Action Step: Consider how well your wealth-building plan protects you from inflation.

Lawsuits: You may as well draw a target on the back of your lab coat; physicians are often the target of lawsuits.

Action Step: Ask yourself, "How vulnerable are my assets?" The more vulnerable, the more likely you are to be named in lawsuits. The more protected your assets are, the better you can sleep at night. Talk with your financial dream team about how you can protect the wealth you've worked so hard to build.

Consider how to protect your wealth against potential financial losses from untoward events in these areas:

- Your home (homeowner's policy with an umbrella)
- Your cars (auto policy)
- Your income (disability, life, critical illness)
- Your clinical activities (medical malpractice, errors and omissions)
- Your health (medical)
- Your accounts receivables
- Your eldercare needs (long-term care insurance)

Other potential lawsuits or financial losses could relate to these areas:

- Identity theft (add an identity theft rider to your home insurance)
- Lawsuits related to employees
- Fraudulent or unethical activity of your partners
- Actions of your children
- Data breaches and PHIPA violations (Personal Health Information Protection Act)

- Telemedicine work
- Social media activity (Technically, posting information on Facebook or Instagram could be viewed as the practice of medicine. Does your medical malpractice policy cover social media activity? If not, look into an errors and omissions policy.)

Financial consequences of the changing health care laws: The financial impact of a changing health care system on hospitals, clinics, and individual practices is still unknown. However, the ability to attend to the business side of medicine could well mean the difference between success and failure.

Market volatility: What happened to your investments in 2008? Does your anxiety go up and down with the market trends? Did you know that there are financial products that allow you to be in the market in a way that you will never lose a dime? The cost for this security is the sacrifice of some of the market gains. After 2008, many physicians feel that this is a small price to pay.

Action Step: Know thyself. Gain greater clarity about your true risk tolerance.

Disability, Illness, or an Early Death: Every day, you work with patients who suddenly and unexpectedly have their lives changed by illness. Our natural tendency is to think, "That happens to patients; we're not vulnerable."

The reality is that one day you could be that patient. Your ability to generate income is your most precious asset. Make sure it's protected.

Action Step: Review your current insurance policies. Make sure that all of the information is up-to-date, especially if you have had a change in your family since you took out the policy. Make sure your will and power of attorney is up-to-date. Discuss your advanced medical and financial directives with family members so they understand what your wishes are. Review your estate plan.

Are Your Beneficiaries Up to Date?

Who are your beneficiaries for your insurance and retirement plans? Many people fail to update their beneficiaries in the event of a divorce or remarriage. Life changes. Make sure you document your plan.

Long-Term Care for You and Your Partner, Your Adult Children, and Your Parents: A Statistics Canada report shows that the number of adults living with a parent has more than doubled. Close to 1.9 million people in Canada—or 9 percent of the adult population aged twenty-five to sixty-four—lived with one or more of their parents in 2017. This was more than double the figure in 1995.

What is your plan for long-term care? Do you know what your parents' plans are? Caring for aging parents is an act of love. It also potentially carries a high emotional cost and huge price tag.

Are You Caring for Aging Parents?

Family caregiving can be one of the most challenging responsibilities you will ever assume—and one of the greatest challenges. This may put pressures on your time, emotions, and finances, and likely on all three.

> ## Money Conversations with Your Aging Parents
>
> How much do you know about your parents' financial health? Finding out means conducting one of the most difficult money conversations you will ever face. Here are a few tips:
>
> 1. Look for natural times to address the subject. If you know friends or family members who are taking on the care of aging parents, talk about it. "I just spoke with Doris, and she stepped into the caregiver role when her father got sick. She told me how grateful she was that her parents had laid out their plan in the event that they could not manage for themselves. Have you and Dad decided what you would like to do if you find yourself in that situation?"
>
> 2. Tell your own story. Say, "Mom and Dad, I am so proud. I just updated my will and advanced directives and durable power of attorney. Have you prepared these documents? What are your wishes?"
>
> 3. Tell the stories of others. If you hear a news story about the cost of eldercare, tell your parents about it

Divorce: Physicians have a lower divorce rate than non–health care professionals (24% versus 40%). Still, the financial consequences of divorce can be devastating. As Robin Williams said, "Ah yes, divorce, from the Latin word meaning to rip out a man's genitals through his wallet." How will you protect your wealth in the event of a divorce? How will you protect your children's legacy in the event that they get divorced?

Money Conversations before You Marry

Oh, the sweetness of having a partner with whom you share life's joys and sorrows. You want to know as much as possible about a person before you decide to spend the rest of your lives together.

Engage in money conversations before you marry! You want to assure your financial compatibility before you begin planning your wedding.

1. Get a read on your betrothed's financial health. Consider going through Part I of this book together.

2. Identify your values and goals. What do you hold most important? What is your vision for your financial future?

3. Formulate a plan for merging money. Consider keeping three bank accounts—yours, mine, and ours. Some couples make a commitment to complete financial transparency, so each member of the couple has access to all three accounts. This minimizes the risk of "financial infidelity."

4. What impact does your partner's family have on your finances? Are you coming from "asymmetric" wealth that might pose stress in the future? Best to deal with it early.

What if you discover that you have fallen in love with an impulsive shopper or someone carrying massive debt? You may still decide to move forward; however, now you're moving forward with open eyes. Consider how you will preserve your own financial health.

While you say "I do" with the hope that your marriage will last forever, the reality is that one in four physicians will find themselves divorced. Talk with your dream team about a contingency plan just in case.

Our National Pastime: Spending

Let's get back to Odysseus's dangerous journey home from the Trojan War. Odysseus knew about the danger of the Siren's song, but he wanted to hear it. He put wax in his men's ears so that they could not hear and had them tie him to the mast so that he could not jump into the sea. He ordered them not to change course under any circumstances and to keep their swords upon him and to attack him if he should break free of his bonds.

Perhaps your greatest danger is succumbing to the siren song of spending. John, whom you met at the beginning of the book, fell under its seductive force and it shipwrecked his family's financial security. He's not alone. We live in a culture of spending and consumption

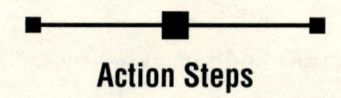

Action Steps

- Assess how well you are protected from these threats and where you are vulnerable.
- Explore whether there are more effective strategies to protect your wealth.
- Revisit your estate plan to make sure it's up-to-date. Look for strategies to help you minimize your estate taxes and pass more to your children and make bigger charitable contributions.

With every choice you make, you move closer to either the illusion of wealth or the reality of wealth.

Spending delays financial freedom in two ways. First, you lose the money you could be saving. Second, you also lose the opportunity to take advantage of the magic of compound interest.

Urban legend holds that Einstein described compound interest as the eighth wonder of the world. Whether or not this is true, these are indeed wise words.

In his book The Elements of Investing, Burton Malkiel tells a story that illustrates the power of compound interest. When Benjamin Franklin died in 1790, he left a gift of $5,000 to each of his two favorite cities: Boston and Philadelphia. He stipulated the money was to be invested, and after 100 years, each city was allowed to draw $500,000 for public works projects. In 1991, the cities could receive the balance. After 200 years, $5,000 had compounded to about $20 million for each city.

As Franklin said, "Money makes money. And the money that money makes, makes money." Sounds like Mr. Wonderful on Shark Tank.

How would you rather build wealth—by seeing more patients or by putting your money to work making money?

Position yourself so that your money gets saved rather than spent. Saved money gets invested, it makes money, and then that money can make even more money.

Action Steps

- Decide what percentage of your income you will save. Automate it. Pay yourself first.

- Control spending by creating an "Odysseus pact." What can you do to put restraints on spending? Tie yourself to the mast. Simple things like eating before grocery shopping impact spending. Explore your triggers for spending. How can you create an environment that supports your dedication to spending less and saving more?

- Help your kids understand your plan. It's never too early to start having money conversations with your kids. Show them how saving more and investing more leads to financial freedom. Ask them how they can contribute to the family savings. Give the kids the amount they saved the family. Help them invest the money, open their own accounts. It's never too early to think about funding your kids' college education. Consider RESPs, if you haven't already done so.

NOTES

NOTES

NOTES

8 THE TEN FINANCIAL HABITS OF WEALTHY PHYSICIANS

Here are the ten financial habits that tend to distinguish thriving physicians from struggling physicians:

1. **Wealthy physicians have clarity about their values and their financial goals.** They are often connected to a purpose bigger than themselves and see their wealth as a way of expanding their legacy. They have a clear sense of the meaning of money in their lives, and their spending reflects their values. They surround themselves with others who share their clarity.

2. **Wealthy physicians have a healthy relationship with money.** They invest time with their money. They treat money with respect. They make informed financial choices. They express gratitude for the privilege of their wealth. They feel comfortable engaging in money conversations, even when it's difficult.

3. **Wealthy physicians know their financial I's and O's.** They do not think of a budget as a punitive burden, but rather as a tool to track financial health.

4. **Wealthy physicians commit to a system of disciplined investing that removes emotion.** The evolving field of behavioral finance offers a harsh financial reality: investors behave irrationally. They make predictable investing errors. Wealthy physicians create an environment that protects them from making these mistakes.

5. **Wealthy physicians embrace tax-efficient investment strategies.** They know that lower taxes are more important than higher returns on investments.

6. **Wealthy physicians see themselves as the leaders of their financial lives.** They assemble a financial dream team and solicit their expert opinions just as you do when you manage the medical care of patients with complex medical conditions. However, just as there is one attending physician of record who assumes ultimate responsibility, likewise, wealthy physicians assume ultimate responsibility for their financial choices.

7. **Wealthy physicians have written financial plans.** They track their progress toward their financial goals. They are prepared to weather financial storms. They plan for the unexpected.

8. **Wealthy physicians ask the right questions.** They understand that the quality of the advice they get is a function of the expertise they seek.

9. **Wealthy physicians vet investment opportunities.** They are willing to take informed risks. They take the long view as they build wealth; they see the difference between minor fluctuations and major trends. They are patient investors; they are not in a rush to build wealth.

10. **Wealthy physicians harness the power of financial leverage.** Think of an investment opportunity as a magic money machine. You watch and see that every time someone feeds a ten-dollar bill into the machine, the machine spits out a twenty or a fifty-dollar bill. Let's say you found a machine that took a ten-dollar bill and spit out a hundred-dollar bill. You would want to do this all day and night! The more you invest, the more money you make. If all of your ten-dollar bills were tied up in another investment, you might be willing to pay two dollars to borrow a ten-dollar bill. After all, after you pay the lender his ten dollars and two-dollar interest, you still make eight dollars (before taxes). You pay to borrow money because the borrowed money helps you make more money. This is leverage.

Thriving Doctors Enjoying Wealth…	Struggling Doctors Living the Myth of the Rich Doctor…
Respect Money	Fear Money
Know Their Financial I's and O's	Guesstimate Their Financial I's and O's
Feel Secure There's Enough	Hope There's Enough
Proactively Engage in Money Conversations	Avoid Money Conversations
Have Control Over Their Money	Find Money Controls Them
Execute a Written Financial Plan	Respond to Financial Crises
Celebrate Their Financial Abundance that Opens Personal and Professional Options	Resent Their Financial Scarcity That Limits Personal and Professional Options
Know Time Is More Important Than Money	Think Money Is More Important Than Time
Spend Intentionally, Guided by Their Values	Spend Impulsively to Impress Others, Alleviate Stress, or Medicate Unwanted Feelings
Have the Financial Freedom to Do What They Want to Do When They Want to Do It	Do What They Need to Pay Their Bills
Seek Expert Advice	Seek Cheap Advice
Create Systems to Automate Saving and Investing	Rely on Willpower to Control Spending and Initiate Investing

Do You Practice Habits of Wealth?

How many of these habits do you currently practice? Which habits will accelerate your ability to achieve financial freedom?

> **Lessons from Mount Everest**
>
> Many want to climb Mount Everest, just like many want to achieve wealth. How and why do climbers die? According to a study published in the BMJ, most deaths occur in the descent. The second most common place of death is at base camp.
>
> Your early career is like the financial base camp. Accumulating wealth is like the ascent, and distribution after retirement is like the descent. The sequencing choices—which financial obligations get funded in which order at the beginning of your career, and the order in which you draw on assets for retirement income—deserve special attention. It can make a huge difference for you!

What Is Your Path to Wealth?

Taking an honest look at your financial health can be difficult. It's also the critical first step in achieving financial freedom. You may be delighted to see that you are in great shape. Or you may see that you have some territory to make up.

Your Choices Got You Here

IIt's important to recognize that your best thinking, decision-making, and investing strategies got you to where you are today. If you want to get different results, you must make changes.

Sometimes the changes are relatively easy to make. You may want to make one small change, like making coffee in the office and at home instead of making daily trips to Starbucks.

Sometimes getting on the path to wealth means making radical, painful changes—firing your trusted office manager who is stealing you blind, putting your kids in public schools, seeing if you really need all the cars you own or lease. It hurts!

Maybe you decide it's time to take the plunge and reinvent your medical practice so you move closer to your personal, professional, and financial goals in the era of changing health care economics.

Change Is Difficult

In his book *Triggers*, executive coach Marshall Goldsmith points out that changing behaviors is one of the hardest things to do. He says that the environment triggers behaviors. If you want to change behaviors, change the environment.

Patients in drug rehabilitation know this. They identify the triggers for their addictive behaviors. Maybe they reach for the vodka bottle when they get together with a certain friend or when they worry about how they will pay the bills or when they have a conflict at work. In order to avoid a relapse, they learn how to avoid the avoidable triggers and respond to the unavoidable triggers in a healthier way.

If you're trying to lose weight, you stock the fridge with healthy food and throw out the unhealthy food so you won't be tempted.

If you want to quit smoking, you identify when you're most likely to reach for a cigarette and make a list of other things you could do instead.

If you think that staying sober or losing weight or giving up cigarettes is difficult, consider this: You formed your relationship with money as a child. Your parents taught you what to do with the check your grandparents sent you on your birthday. Your patterns of spending, saving, and investing are almost as old as you are.

Change Is Possible

Once you decide that building wealth is important to you, you can replace your wealth-eroding money habits with wealth-building money habits. Even though it's hard, you can do it. You had the discipline to get through medical school and residency!

> **Lessons from the Ski Slope**
>
> You may have read one of Bonnie St. John's books or heard her speak. Despite having her right leg amputated at age five, she became the first African American ever to win Olympic or Paralympic medals in ski racing. She tells her story about racing in the 1984 Paralympics. She was confident that she would win, so she encouraged her family members to travel to Austria to see her take home the gold.
>
> She was making excellent time on her run when she hit some tricky moguls and fell. She describes lying in the snow feeling horrified, devastated, and embarrassed. Not only did she fail, she failed in front of her family. She knew she could not stay on the slope, so she got herself up and crossed the finish line.
>
> Later, she learned that every athlete fell at that point in the run. The slower athlete who won gold just got up more quickly than she did.

Explore How Well Your Current Team Is Serving You

You have the intellectual prowess to master investing.

Here are some questions for your consideration:

- How many hours a week can you reasonably invest in wealth building?
- How many conferences about wealth building can you attend in a year?
- How well can you detach yourself from your emotions and avoid the common investing mistakes our species is known to make?
- How do you think the results that you get building your portfolio compare with the results an advisor with thirty years in financial services would get?

You know that experience correlates with results. The surgeon who performs ten Whipples a month will likely get better clinical outcomes than a colleague who does five a year.

Here are the titles of experts wealthy physicians include on their financial dream team:

- Accountant
- Financial advisor/wealth manager
- Estate planner
- Tax lawyer
- Insurance experts

Choosing team members is much like dating; it's all about goodness of fit.

How to Identify Team Members You Can Trust

When physician financial do-it-yourselfers were asked, "Why don't you work with a professional financial advisor?" the most common answer was, "I can't find someone I can trust."

This begs the question: "Trust to do what?" Put your interests first? Be knowledgeable about all the investing options? Be a person of integrity who conducts herself or himself ethically? Beat the market?

Financial advisors come in many "flavors." Some conduct themselves professionally and others less so.

Clearly you want to work with the former and avoid the latter. How do you do that?

Action Steps

Get the names of potential dream team members from colleagues you trust.

Interview potential team members and listen carefully. Ask yourself the ten deciding questions that follow in this chapter.

You might hear, "Look at the advisor's fee structure, and avoid advisors who collect commissions. You don't want them to have a financial incentive for pushing product."

We respectfully disagree. You get fees for your services. Does this mean that you make treatment recommendations based on your ability to optimize your fees? Absolutely not! You made a commitment to putting the needs of your patients first, and your professional ethics and personal integrity guide your actions.

How do you assess the ethics and integrity of an advisor? It can be difficult. That's why a recommendation from someone you trust is so valuable.

Some physicians want to work with the advisor with the lowest fees. You should absolutely scrutinize investing fees and inquire about hidden fees in any financial product. However, I will also point out that in the high-stakes financial services industry, fees often correlate with outcomes. If you needed plastic surgery, would you choose the surgeon with the lowest fees?

Look at the ROI—your return on investment—instead of fees. Would you rather spend $10 for advice that puts $100 in your pocket, or $1 to make $1.25?

Some physicians say, "I'm looking for someone who can beat the market." Please allow me to point out that in Vegas the house always wins; this is a statistical certainty. Chasing the market is like trying to beat Vegas; your most probable outcome is a net loss.

Deciding Questions

Here are the questions to ask when choosing consultants and advisors:

1. Do they understand me? How many clients like me do they have?

2. Do they listen to me? Do they begin by learning more about who I am and what's important to me, or do they begin by telling me ten reasons I should work with them?

3. Do they diagnose before they treat? You diagnose before you treat; so should your advisor.

4. What is their net worth? Would you rather get wealth-building advice from advisors who have built wealth for themselves, or advisors who are struggling?

5. Do they personally use the financial products and strategies they are recommending to me? If not, why not?

6. Do they have an active working knowledge of the risks and benefits of all of the financial products? Can they explain why they are recommending one financial product over another and support their point of view with evidence?

7. Do they offer absolute transparency? Is my money held with a third-party custodian? Can I see with my own eyes exactly what is happening in my portfolio?

8. Do they tell the truth all the time? Little white lies are red flags.

9. Do they accept responsibility and remain accountable if they make a mistake? We all make mistakes; it's part of the human condition. Do the advisors have checklists and systems to minimize the risk of mistakes?

10. What does my gut say?

Ask the Best Questions

The quality of your financial knowledge is shaped by the quality of questions you ask. Here are some questions for your consideration, which you might consider answering in written detail:

How do I build wealth? (accumulating assets)

What are the most effective investment strategies for me at different stages of my career? In other words, how do I put my money to work making money?

What are the asset classes, and which mix is best for me? (asset allocation)

What's the best way to leverage my own money and other people's money?

How do I keep more of what I have? (plugging wealth leaks)

How do I legally and ethically minimize my tax burden now and in retirement?

How do I protect my wealth—including my home—in the event of lawsuits? (asset protection)

How can the creation of legal corporate entities protect my wealth, and which is the best choice for me?

How do I avoid losing money? (avoiding losses)

How do I minimize the impact of market losses at various stages of my career?

How do I assess investment opportunities I learn about in the doctors' dining room and surgeons' lounge?

How will I protect myself from fraud, theft, and embezzlement?

In retirement, how do I access my money? (distributing assets)

How do I decide what assets generate revenue and in what order?

How will I make sure I don't outlive my money?

How will I protect my family if I cannot practice medicine?

What will happen to my family if I die too soon or become disabled?

How will eldercare be funded? (for my parents, my spouse, and myself)

Who could sue me?

What kinds of insurance do I need?

How do I protect my wealth in the event of divorce?

How will I pass my wealth to others? (creating a legacy)

After I die, how do I pass my wealth on to my children and minimize estate taxes? (intergenerational wealth transfer)

How do I protect my children's inheritance in the event of their divorce? (prenuptial agreements)

How do I make my philanthropic contributions go the furthest?

How do I run my practice? (operational optimization)

How do I assess clinical practice opportunities? What do I look for in partners and colleagues?

What should I do before I sign a contract?

How will I protect myself from unethical or illegal misconduct of my partners?

How do I customize my financial plan for my current financial life stage?

You will face different challenges at different stages of your career. This makes sense. Kids have different medical needs than pregnant women, seniors, or immunocompromised patients. Ask yourself: What should I be thinking about today? Five years from now? Ten years from now? At different stages of my life?

Answer Day-to-Day Questions

How do I raise financially literate children?

How much house can I afford?

What are the pros and cons of buying a vacation home?

Should I buy or lease a car?

Should I pay off my house early?

What's the best way to pay for my kids' education?

Explore How Well Your Current Investing Strategy Is Serving You

Just as there are new diagnostic and therapeutic tools to help you take better care of patients, there are also new financial tools that can help you build wealth more effectively. Sometimes you can build wealth by using an old product in a new way. For example, there are financial products that can help you do the following:Minimize your taxes

- Minimize your taxes
- Protect your wealth from creditors
- Gain tax-free retirement income
- Leave a death benefit
- Protect yourself from market losses

Getting Unstuck from Conventional Wisdom

It's humbling to take a look at medical history and understand that conventional wisdom often turns out to be wrong.

First, Do No Harm. Medical historians believe that George Washington died of strep pharyngitis. His physicians treated him with state-of-the-art medical care for that time: bleeding and purging. By today's standards, we would say his doctors harmed the president. Today he could have been cured with a dose of antibiotics unknown at his time.

Get It Right. Peptic ulcers were once thought to be caused by excess acid. Get rid of the acid and get rid of the ulcers. That's what we were taught in medical school.

Around that same time, Drs. Warren and Marshall suggested that ulcers were caused by an infection with H. pylori. Get rid of the bacteria and get rid of the ulcers. It took over forty years to change the standard of care, even though the new model offered a safer, easier path to the desired outcome. These physicians were awarded a Nobel Prize for their contributions.

Notice Happy Coincidences. You know the story of Alexander Fleming's "discovery" of penicillin. He noticed that a petri dish containing staphylococcus that had been mistakenly left open was contaminated by blue-green bread mold. Fleming observed a halo of inhibited bacterial growth around the mold. He concluded that the mold released a substance that repressed the growth of the bacteria.

Do you know the Viagra story? Originally, Pfizer was testing a drug called sildenafil, the active drug in Viagra, to treat hypertension. At the end of the trial, the men did not want to give the medication back. Why not? They were enjoying the drug's "side effect"—erections that allowed them to perform as they did in their younger days.

Similar stories can be told about wealth-building financial interventions.

Consider Seeking a Second Opinion

What would you do if you were caring for a complex patient who was not responding to treatment as expected? Chances are good that you would start from scratch and challenge the assumptions that you have made.

You have complex financial needs. What are the benchmarks for discerning whether you are taking the best path to optimal financial health? Are you ahead? Are you behind?

Further, what is your level of certainty that you are using investment strategies that are right for you? Are you basing your financial decisions on conventional investing dogma for the average Canadian that may or may not address your unique financial needs?

These are difficult questions to answer. Second opinions can help you look in your blind spots and challenge assumptions that may be holding you back.

It's Never Too Late

You may think it's too late to achieve financial independence.

Years ago, families that could not conceive a child, were facing very few options. Adoption, which should never be discounted, was often their only option. With modern medicine, IVF and third-party donation has brought forth many new solutions.

If you are in your fifties and cannot conceive of retirement in your future, new financial products and services could be like your financial IVF.

It's Never Too Early

You may think it's too early to achieve financial independence, or to start thinking about investment goals. If you are a medical student, resident, or early in your medical career, you are likely in the best position to set your financial health in gear. Establishing your financial goals early, becoming an informed consumer, and building your dream team will pay you countless dividends in the years to come.

NOTES

NOTES

NOTES

AFTERWORD: A CALL TO ACTION

Thank you for investing your time in exploring the wealth-building ideas in this book. We hope that you found value in this information and have gained a deeper understanding about doctors and their relationship with money. We also hope that you will treat yourself with more compassion now that you have more insights about how and why physicians make financial choices.

As you well know, insight alone will not lead to transformation. This requires action. Think about one action step that called to you as you read the book, and take it! One small step leads to another and another.

Please feel welcome to visit www.TheMythoftheRichDoctor.ca and get your complimentary copy of "Your Financial I's and O's" to get a better handle on the state of your current financial health. Share your financial story. The website will also be a source of continuous learning for you and a way for us to continue providing you with new ideas and thoughts.

No matter where you are today, you can make a plan to enjoy a more hopeful tomorrow.

Our wish for you is that you see a more hopeful future and create the financial foundation that will allow you to return to the joy that attracted you to a career in medicine.

What did you think of the ideas in this book? We welcome you to reach out with your thoughts or questions or concerns. It is through conversations with physicians like you that we are in the best position to offer you these ideas

ACKNOWLEDGMENTS

[From Dr. Michael Varenbut]

First and foremost, I thank Dr. Vicki Rackner for her hard work and dedication to this book and to the overall mission of working with professionals (such as investment advisors, lawyers, and insurance specialists) to improve the lives of physicians. I further thank Vicki for allowing me to collaborate with her on this Canadian edition of the book and to invite Canadian physicians and professionals working with them to benefit from the wisdom of the text. The Canadian health care system is unique, and it was my goal to address this uniqueness in my approach to the Canadian edition.

I would not have been able to complete this project without the ongoing and ever-present support from my true rock and confidant, my wife, Lori. I am eternally grateful for her presence in my life. My daughters, Elysha and Jaymie, have been instrumental as my "sounding board" during the writing of this book, and I thank them both for their raw input and editorial contributions. I also thank my sister, Nirit, for her keen eye for details and linguistic skills.

[From Dr. Vicki] The work of creation is messy. I want to thank the many people who have given from their hearts to help me transform vague notions in my head into the words you hold in your hands.

First, a huge thanks to the many medical colleagues who trusted me with their stories. Many physicians told their financial truths for the first time. I admire your courage!

I also extend my gratitude to my financial advisor clients who have taught me so much about how money works.

Thank you to the people and organizations who invited me to contribute to their publications, speak at their meetings, and appear on their radio shows.

A special thanks to my friends, family, and community who have supported me in a time of transition. My son, Meir, continues to be my eternal source of joy and inspiration. And while writing is a solitary activity, I'm never alone. My dog is my constant companion, reminding me of the bumper sticker that says, "Lord, help me to be the person my dog thinks I am."

ABOUT THE AUTHORS

Michael Varenbut, MD, MBA. For more than twenty-five years, alongside his career in medicine, Dr. Varenbut has been involved in the founding and operation of medical clinics, companies, and collaborations. He has also been involved in both active and passive investments in various sectors and industries for the past twenty years.

This was, in part, a catalyst behind his decision to pursue business endeavors in a more official capacity and return to school, this time to study business. In 2018, he graduated with distinction from Ivey Business School with his MBA.

Now, he wants to combine his experience in health care with his business knowledge and training to be able to help other professionals interact with physicians in ways that will benefit all stakeholders.

Vicki Rackner, MD, FACS calls on her thirty-plus-year medical career as a practicing surgeon, as clinical faculty at the University of Washington School of Medicine, and serial entrepreneur to help her doctor clients thrive.

A nationally noted author, speaker, and consultant, Dr. Vicki builds the bridge between the world of business and the world of medicine. She's the expert quoted in publications ranging from the Wall Street Journal, Washington Post, and Physician Money Digest, to name a few. She is the author of multiple books, including The New Thriving Medical Practice.

CNN Senior Medical Correspondent Elizabeth Cohen says, "Don't miss Dr. Vicki Rackner."